# When Early
# an

**Dick B.'s Reference Titles on Alcoholics Anonymous History**
**Paradise Research Publications, Inc., Publisher;**
**Good Book Publishing Company, Distributor** P.O. Box 837, Kihei, HI 96753-0837
Phone/Fax: (808) 874 4876; Email: dickb@dickb.com; URL: http://www.dickb.com/index.shtml
**Publisher's December 1, 2005 List of Titles by Author Dick B.; All list prices: Effective December 1, 2005**

*Anne Smith's Journal, 1933-1939*, 3rd ed.; 1998; 6 x 9; 180 pp.; $16.95
*By the Power of God: A Guide to Early A.A. Groups & Forming Similar Groups Today*; 2000, 6 x 9; 260 pp., $16.95
*Cured!: Proven Help for Alcoholics and Addicts*; 2003, 6 x 9; 182 pp., $17.95
*Dr. Bob and His Library*, 3rd ed.; 1998; 6 x 9; 156 pp.; $15.95
*God and Alcoholism: Our Growing Opportunity in the 21st Century*; 2002; 6 x 9; 190 pp.; $17.95
*Good Morning!: Quiet Time, Morning Watch, Meditation, and Early A.A.*; 2d ed.; 1998; 6 x 9; 154 pp.; $16.95
*Henrietta B. Seiberling: Ohio's Lady with a Cause,* Rev. ed.; 2004; 46 pp.; 8 ½ x 11; spiral bound, $15.95
*Making Known The Biblical History and Roots of Alcoholics Anonymous: An Eleven-Year Research, Writing, Publishing and Fact Dissemination Project*, 2001, 160 pp., spiral bound, $24.95
*New Light on Alcoholism: God, Sam Shoemaker, and A.A.*; 2d ed.; 1999; 6 x 9; 672 pp.; $24.95
*The Akron Genesis of Alcoholics Anonymous*, 2d ed.; 1998; 6 x 9; 400 pp.; $17.95
*The Books Early AAs Read for Spiritual Growth*, 7th ed.; 1998; 6 x 9; 126 pp.; $15.95
*The First Nationwide A.A. History Conference - Comments of Dick B.*, 2003, 8 ½ x 11, 79 pp., spiral bound, $17.95
*The Golden Text of A.A.: God, the Pioneers, and Real Spirituality*; 1999; 6 x 9; 76 pp.; $14.95
*The Good Book and The Big Book: A.A.'s Roots in the Bible*; 2d ed.; 1997; 6 x 9; 264 pp.; $17.95
*The James Club: The Original A.A. Program's Absolute Essentials, 3rd ed.*, 2005; 6 x 9; $17.95
*The Oxford Group & Alcoholics Anonymous*, 2d ed.; 1998; 6 x 9; 432 pp.; $17.95
*That Amazing Grace* (Clarence & Grace S.); 1996; 6 x 9; 160 pp.; $16.95

*Turning Point: A History of Early A.A.'s Spiritual Roots and Successes;* 1997; 6 x 9; 776 pp.; $29.95

*Twelve Steps for You: Let Our Creator, A.A. History, and the Big Book Be Your Guide*; 2003; 6 x 9; 90 pp. $17.95

*Utilizing Early A.A.'s Spiritual Roots for Recovery Today*; Rev. ed.; 1999; 6 x 9; 106 pp., $14.95

*When Early AA s Were Cured and Why*; 2003; 8 ½ x 11; spiral bound; 114 pp.; $17.95

*Why Early A.A. Succeeded: The Good Book in Alcoholics Anonymous Yesterday and Today* (a Bible Study Primer), 2001; 6 x 9; 340 pp., $17.95

**Available through other distributors**

*Hope: The Story of Geraldine O. Delaney*, 2d ed. NJ: Alina Lodge

*Our Faith Community A.A. Legacy* (Dick B., ed and compiler). FL: Came to Believe Publications

*Courage to Change* (with Bill Pittman). MN: Hazelden

*Women Pioneers of AA* (Dick B., contributor). MN: Hazelden

# When Early AAs Were Cured and Why

**Dick B.**

Historian, Bible Student, Retired Attorney, Recovered AA
(Author of 26 Titles on Early A.A.'s Spiritual Roots)

**Paradise Research Publications, Inc.**
**Kihei, Maui, Hawaii**

**Paradise Research Publications, Inc.**
P.O. Box 837
Kihei, HI 96753-0837
(808) 874-4876
Email: dickb@dickb.com
URL: http://www.dickb.com/index.shtml


Published 2003, 2005, 2006
Printed in the United States of America

This Paradise Research Publications Edition is published by arrangement with Good Book Publishing Company, PO Box 837, Kihei, HI: 96753-0837

Cover Design: Terry Dunford (American Creations of Maui)



Note: All Bible verses quoted in this book, unless otherwise noted, are from the Authorized (or "King James") Version. The letters "KJV" are used when necessary to distinguish it from other versions.

ISBN 1-885803-94-X

# Contents

# Introduction

In 1990, it became apparent to me that the early history of A.A. had reached a new and different level. For several decades, revisionists had sold A.A. publishing people, many A.A. members, and a good many recovery publishers on what amounted to half a history. In 1990, I began a search for the other "half." The other half turned out to be far more than half, and that large–much larger–portion had been ignored, misrepresented, distorted, and–for the most part–simply omitted from every significant writing about A.A. history. As the research marched on, piece by piece, I was able to establish first the existence and importance of Dr. Bob's Library. Then the existence and importance of Anne Smith's Journal. Then the tremendous significance of the Oxford Group, even though it had taken a bad rap from Bill Wilson and a good many other A.A. members, not to mention the Roman Catholic Church and lots of historians. Then came the special role of Rev. Sam Shoemaker as friend, mentor, and actual teacher of Bill Wilson, not to mention all the literature Shoemaker had written and which was devoured by early A.A. members. At last came the Bible–the most ignored and yet fundamental root of early A.A. ideas. Finally, the Christian literature and devotionals that the pioneers had read, primarily in Akron. And then, when I felt I had been able to piece the entire picture together, it seemed that A.A.'s roots could be described as six major Biblical roots–the Bible, Quiet Time, Anne Smith's Journal, the teachings of Rev. Sam Shoemaker, the life-changing program of the Oxford Group, and the Christian literature that early A.A. members and families read.

So much for that neat package! Some critics were saying I was a prime-mover in an effort to Christianize A.A. Some were saying I had left out Sister Ignatia and Father Dowling. Some were saying that neither the Bible nor the Oxford Group had "worked" for Dr. Bob and should be discarded from A.A. Some even said that all the original A.A. people died drunk, and that people would get drunk if they studied the early history–particularly the Bible and the Oxford Group. Some groups were banning Bible study, Christian literature, and meetings studying such matters.

But several errors were being made: (1) The first was my own. There was simply more research to be done. It involved the roles and beliefs of Carl Jung, William James, William Silkworth, Richard Peabody, and New Thought writers. (2) Second, there was my growing realization that there was a distinct difference between the A.A. that was developed in Akron, and the A.A. that Bill Wilson fashioned in his Big Book--a difference in roots, a difference in mentors, a difference in beliefs, a difference in program, a difference in audience, and a difference in successes. For Akron's program was highly successful–producing a 75% to 93% documented success rate; and Wilson's program was a flop for the first four years and–over the passage of time–had an increasingly miserable success rate of 1% to 5%. (3) Third, after extensive initial research, I realized that the Akron program stemmed far more from the United Christian Endeavor Society of Dr. Bob's youth–with emphasis on confession of Christ, Bible study, prayer meetings, Quiet Hour, conversion meetings, fellowship, witness, love and service. This while the New York program eventually codified the life-changing program of the Oxford Group and bore little resemblance to the "old fashioned prayer meetings" of the little group of alcoholics and Oxford Group people in Akron who were bent on helping drunks. (4) Then came the startling discovery that, for its first decade of existence, A.A., its founders, and its people uniformly claimed they had been *cured* of alcoholism–only to see this "cure" idea erased *sub silencio* by an apparent handful of later, non-pioneer A.A. writers. And the reasons behind this erasure were far less significant than the hole its absence had left in recovery. From a certain point, A.A. began saying outright or in effect: "Condemned, not cured;" "Once an alcoholic always an alcoholic," and "There is no cure for alcoholism."

There's lots more to this myth-making. But, by the time I got these things under my belt and began to write and speak about them, I found that some 150,000 of my books were in print, that my website had exceeded 390,000 visitors just since 1995, and that I was being inundated with letters, emails, phone calls, and personal visits by those who were hungry for the truth–hungry to know all the details about early A.A. and the Bible, Dr. Bob's books, Anne Smith's Journal, the real Oxford Group picture, the role of Rev. Shoemaker, and Quiet Time–not to mention the other significant roots.

The end result was, in addition to my continued research and writing, The First Nationwide Alcoholics Anonymous History Conference, held in Phoenix, Arizona, and devoted to allowing an accurate presentation by a substantial group of qualified speakers of our history to the A.A. members at large throughout the United States. It was a first. Dr. Bob's son gave what I believe was his last historical talk to an history-hungry audience. Ray G., archivist at Dr. Bob's Home, came with all his books, articles, exhibits, manuscripts, and other early treasures and conducted a workshop. And I was permitted to lay out the materials that are covered in my title on that first conference. See Dick B., *The First Nationwide Alcoholics Anonymous History Conference*, 2d ed. Kihei, HI: Paradise Research Publications, Inc., 2006

Then there was clamor, by the people who had been attending my annual heritage seminars at The Wilson House, to have a similar nationwide A.A. history conference on the East Coast. And this was held in Wilmington, Delaware in August of 2003. The speaker panel was expanded. Ray G. was there from Dr. Bob's Home. Richard K.–who had been devoting himself to research of all the "cure" literature and of the actual successes of A.A.'s "First Forty Pioneers"–was there to speak, to present his three newly written books on the cure story and the pioneers. Dr. Karen Plavan, who had taken a special interest in the role of Dr. Shoemaker, gave a presentation on Shoemaker's A.A. role. Veronica R., a talented researcher and writer and teacher, worked up a presentation of three women starlets of the pioneer scene–Anne Smith, Henrietta Seiberling, and Clarace Williams. And I gave the remaining talks–most of whose contents are set forth below.

It seemed important to turn the second conference materials into a book. And this is that book. Here's what the Delaware conference heard–and more!

# 1

# What They Were Saying at Yale

## The Yale Summer School of Alcohol Studies

The Yale Summer School of Alcohol Studies began in 1943. It was an experiment in social education. The purpose was to put before the students–most of whom were professional social workers, ministers, and temperance educators, as well as school and college teachers–the facts and theories in their integration. The school's director, Howard W. Haggard, stated by way of introduction that the problem of alcoholism has medical, social, legal, educational, and religious factors. And it still does!

In 1944, twenty-nine lectures by men from various institutions were selected for publication. The lectures were published in a text that has frequently been quoted in ensuing years: *Alcohol, Science and Society: Twenty-nine Lectures with Discussions as given at the Yale Summer School of Alcohol Studies* (New Haven: Quarterly Journal of Studies on Alcohol, 1945).

Among the published lectures was that by A.A. co-founder Bill Wilson, whose remarks have since been published by A.A. itself. Our discussion here will concern the cure of alcoholism claimed and achieved by early AAs and their Christian Fellowship, but some of the observations by the Yale lecturers will highlight the miraculous cures accomplished in Akron between 1935 and 1939.

## The Lecture of the Reverend Francis W. Mc Peek

Reverend Mc Peek was the Executive Director of the Federation of Churches in Washington, D.C. He said:

> It is, moreover, the insistence of historical Christianity that no man can live fully without a knowledge of and dependence upon God. . . . No one is exempt (p. 404).

The deep-running desires for a faith which united and heals the soul and directs the will, and the bits of emotionally tinged knowledge of God from earlier times, are refreshed or activated in many ways. Sometimes they are strengthened by chance words heard or real–a phrase overheard from conversation in a public place, a radio sermon, a service of public worship, a quotation from the Scriptures in an unexpected place. Augustine was converted by reading a single passage; St. Anthony by a single word (p. 405).

But by all odds the most of those who find their way back to sobriety after years of indulgence find it because they first find a friend with whom there is no necessity of pretense. The scold, the crank, the moralizer, the contemptuous–these serve usually only to widen the abyss, already so great, that separates the inebriate from those to whom he most truly wishes to belong. The hallmark of a good friend is his stability and freedom from censoriousness; the hallmark of a religious friend is not only these things, but also a humility tempered with unshaken faith. To these religious elements we add one other–the moving power of mass example (pp. 405-406).

For his audience, Mc Peek had reviewed what he called "a brief and highly selective survey of a century's efforts among religious people to bring the healing power of God into the lives of those who suffer from inebriety." He had discussed the American Temperance Society (1827), Washington Temperance Society (1840), Father Matthew in Ireland (1838), the great revival work of Moody and Sankey (1877), the Salvation Army, the Emmanuel Clinic, and Courtenay Baylor.

Then, probably without realizing it, Mc Peek discussed the technique of the Salvation Army and really laid out the very program which Akron A.A. itself had used in the 1930's. At pages 414-415, he said, concerning the Salvation Army techniques:

Much work was done in city missions and particularly by the Salvation Army. The Army, however, has focused its efforts on the conversion experience and has made use of its own general facilities and of other community resources when these were needed in aftercare. Those who wish to read a portrayal of the Salvation Army's methods and approach may consult Hall's biography of Henry F. Milans (*Out of the Depth*).

Generally speaking, the **Salvationists have capitalized on the same techniques that have made other reform programs work**: (1) **Insistence on total abstinence** [the primary Akron requirement]. (2) **reliance on God** [the first requirement offered to the Akronite as he left the hospital]. (3) the provision of

**new friendships among those who understand** [the "social and religious comradeship" which characterized the Akron Christian Fellowship]. (4) **the opportunity to work with those who suffer from the same difficulty** [the epitome of Dr. Bob's stance as Prince of Twelfth Steppers, and the work in hospitals]. (5) unruffled patience and **consistent faith in the ability of the individual and in the power of God to accomplish the desired ends** [the whole Akron program of living with the Smiths and others, attending morning Quiet Time with Anne Smith, reading Christian literature, and engaging in ceaseless Bible study, prayer, conversions, fellowship, and witness highlighted this technique] (bold face added)

We should add that Mc Peek missed a good many references, particularly to individual healers throughout the centuries, who had brought about cures through the power of God. Nonetheless, Mc Peek provided the following powerful message at page 417:

> Certain things may be held as conclusive. **Towering above them all is this indisputable fact: It is faith in the living God which has accounted for more recoveries from the disease than all other therapeutic agencies put together** [bold face added].

## The Lecture of the Reverend Dr. Otis R. Rice

Reverend Otis R. Rice, Ph.D., Religious Director, St. Luke's Hospital, New York, was another clergyman who addressed the Yale school. He had these things to add at pp. 445-446:

> . . . the use of the word of God with alcoholics is important. . . the word of God in its revelation of Divine concern for the individual can often bring the alcoholic back into a feeling that his life is worth while even though he has lost his self-belief and those around him have lost their belief in him.
>
> We are miserable sinners. We begin from that point. We have fallen far short of what God would have us be. We have gone far astray from our close relationship with God, and by our sinfulness have departed from our close union with God. . . . The other half of the doctrine of man is that we are potential sons of God. **It is from the fact that one is a miserable sinner, and the acceptance of the fact that by God's promise one can become His son, that cures are made and that lives are made worthwhile** [emphasis added].

## The Lecture of A.A.'s William Griffith Wilson

Bill Wilson's lecture was the last of those reported (pp. 461-470). Bill told the scholars about his sponsor Ebby Thacher who had achieved a cure and had come to help drunken Bill–still in his cups. Ebby had said to Bill: "Well, I've got religion." Ebby further explained his victory over alcohol with the flat declaration that God had done for him what he could not do for himself–a statement quoted several times in the text Bill wrote in the Big Book. Ebby then challenged an argumentative Bill to achieve the same liberation. To Bill, Ebby had explicitly said:

> **So, call on God as you understand God. Try prayer** [emphasis added].

According to Bill, he [Bill] "humbly" did just that. For Bill, the result was his so-called "hot flash" experience he recounted hundreds and hundreds of times for later AAs. In a variety of statements, he described his experience in calling for help: The following is a synopsis of quotes:

> I remember saying to myself, "I'll do anything, anything at all. If there be a Great Physician, I'll call on him." Then, with neither faith nor hope I cried out, "If there be a God, let him show himself." Then came a sudden experience in which it seemed the room lit up. It felt [said Bill] as though I stood on the top of a mountain, that a great clean wind blew, that I was free. [Elsewhere, Bill wrote that he had exclaimed:] **"This," I thought, "must be the great reality. The God of the preachers." . . . . For sure I'd been born again** (emphasis added.) See and compare: *Bill W.: My First 40 Years* (Center City, MN: Hazelden, 2000), pp. 145-47; *Pass It On* (NY: Alcoholics Anonymous World Services, 1984), p. 121].

Bill Wilson had thus "found God"–as Rev. Sam Shoemaker so often taught was possible and necessary. Wilson had "acted as if" in accordance with the following typical Shoemaker suggestions:

> Behave and live as if God were, and you will find that He is. Reach out to Him in every way open to you, and He will make Himself known to you [Sam Shoemaker. *Extraordinary Living for Ordinary Men* (Grand Rapids, MI: Zondervan Publishing House, 1965), p. 28].

> The crux of it will lie in whether. . . you bring them to real decision and surrender to Christ. They may not be able to make a statement that they understand the whole of the Christian faith as yet, but any honest person can begin the spiritual experiment by surrendering "as much of

himself as he can, to as much of Christ as he understands" [Shoemaker, *Extraordinary Living, supra*, p. 76].

> The romance of religion is the romance of a risk. Some of us have flung everything we have got into it. There are only two alternatives here–God is, or He isn't. You leap one way or the other. It is a risk to take, to bet everything you have on God. So is it a risk not to. . . . Do you want the romance of real religion? Then pay the price of real religion. Let your life go into the hands of God [Shoemaker, *Extraordinary Living, supra*, p. 21].

Bill stuck to the Shoemaker language and with Shoemaker's suggested experiment of faith based on what was said to be Sam's favorite Bible verse:

> John 7:17:
> If any man will do his will, he shall know of the doctrine, whether it be of God, or whether I speak of myself.

Bill adhered to that idea of Sam's for years, and long after Bill's own "hot flash" risk adventure. Bill wrote in his own basic text:

> When we became alcoholics, crushed by a self-imposed crisis we could not postpone or evade, we had to fearlessly face the proposition that either God is everything or else He is nothing. God either is, or He isn't. What was our choice to be? . . . He humbly offered himself to His Maker–then he knew. . . . When we drew near to Him, He disclosed Himself to us! [*Alcoholics Anonymous*, 4th ed, 2001, pp. 53-57].

Note that Bill Wilson had used Shoemaker's experiment of faith before there ever was an A.A. Thus, in his Towns Hospital surrender, Bill had called on God *as Bill understood God*. This surrender had occurred after Bill's long discussions with his physician Dr. William Duncan Silkworth about the "Great Physician" Jesus Christ and the healings that were available through turning to this Great Physician (See Dale Mitchel, *Silkworth: The Little Doctor Who Loved Drunks*. MN: Hazelden, 2002, pp. 46-48, 50-52, 225, 96, 106, 159-160).

The "conservative atheist" believed he had then "found" God. And that former atheist, Bill Wilson, proclaimed clearly that he had been cured. He often said so many times in the beginning years of A.A.

Bill's Yale lecture was equally explicit as to another miracle which concerned Jim Burwell–a man whom AAs have since been led to believe was an atheist. To be sure, Burwell had more than once said in A.A. meetings: "But I don't like this God business." And "Damn this God business." In fact, we hear that kind of talk in A.A. meetings to this day. But Burwell went back to his drinking and a mean drunken period. Then the miracle occurred, which Bill Wilson described as follows to his Yale audience (pp. 467-468):

> . . . [I]t appeared that over in that little second-rate hotel he [Jim Burwell] had nearly died from the worst seizure he had ever had, and something in him had given way. I think it is just what gave way in me. It was his prideful obstinacy. He had thought to himself: "Maybe these fellows have got something with their God-business." His hand reached out, in the darkness, and touched something on his bureau. It was a Gideon Bible. Jimmy picked it up and he read from it. I do not know just what he read, and I have always had a queer reluctance to ask him. But Jimmy has not had a drink to this day, and that was about 5 years ago.

Thus another self-proclaimed "atheist" had "found God." He hadn't found a light bulb. He hadn't found a goddess. He hadn't found a door knob. What Jim Burwell had found, in his drunken stupor, was a Gideon Bible–which doesn't teach about light bulbs or "somethings" or "someones" or "higher powers" or "not-god-ness." It gave Jim Burwell enough of an understanding of, and belief in, the Creator to effect the very cure by the true and living God about whom he had been hearing. Jim's discovery of his hopelessness and his going to God as a last resort reminds me of an old A.A. expression which is heard quite frequently to this day:

> If the word "God" drives you out of these rooms, a bottle of booze will drive you back if you live that long [See. Dick B., *That Amazing Grace: The Role of Clarence and Grace S. in A.A.* (San Rafael, CA: Paradise Research Publications, 1996), p. 89].

Bill explained to the Yale audience A.A.'s progress from its founding in the summer of 1935, declaring (p. 466):

> This wonderful blessing that has come to us, from what does it get its origin? It was a spiritual awakening growing out of painful adversity. So then we began to look the harder for our mistakes, to correct them, to capitalize upon our errors. And little by little we began to grow so that there were 5 of us at the end of that first year [1935]; at the end of

> the second year, 15 [1936]; at the end of the third year, 40 [1937]; at the end of the fourth year, 100 [1938]–
> [The reader should note that the purported 1938 statistic is highly suspect even if Bill was referring to a full year which ended with the publication of the Big Book in the Spring of 1939].

Let's review the process Bill was explaining to the Yale school. At about the same time as the time of his lecture, Bill had been on the platform in Los Angeles with Dr. Bob, stating that the process involved "Divine Aid." The actual results of this Divine Aid? It's hard to tell the precise numbers, but Bill's tally meant that there were five cures in a year, fifteen cures by the end of two years, and by other estimates something over seventy by the end of the third full year. Those cured had almost all been pronounced "medically" incurable. They were believed to be in "seemingly hopeless" conditions. They included the "last gasp" real alcoholics who had really tried. They had been transformed by reliance on the Creator. And they confidently and consistently said that they were cured–cured by the "Lord." They had found a cure for alcoholism that astonished them and enabled them to take a miraculous offer to drunks the world over.

## The Point?–The Miracle of God's Cure became the "Golden Text of A.A."

Let's hear from Bill W. how he looked at his miracle from God:

> Henrietta, the Lord has been so wonderful to me, curing me of this terrible disease, that I just want to keep talking about it and telling people (*Alcoholics Anonymous*, 4th ed. New York: Alcoholics Anonymous World Services, 2001, p. 191).

Bill's thankful partner and co-founder Dr. Bob said:

> It is a most wonderful blessing to be relieved of the terrible curse with which I was afflicted. . . . I spend a great deal of time passing on what I learned to others who want and need it badly. . . . Your Heavenly Father will never let you down! (*Alcoholics Anonymous*, 4th ed., *supra*, pp. 180-81).

Bill Dotson, who was called A.A. Number Three, and was the first success in the new program then being developed by Bill W. and Dr. Bob, heard and quoted Bill Wilson's remark and said of his (Dotson's) own cure:

> That sentence, "The Lord has been so wonderful to me, curing me of this terrible disease, that I just want to keep telling people about it," has been a sort of golden text for the A.A. program and for me (*Alcoholics Anonymous*, 4th ed., *supra*, p. 191).

That, then, was the golden text of the A.A. *of yesteryear*. Reliance on God can produce, did produce, and will produce miraculous cures for those suffering from alcoholism and other addictions. That can and should be the golden text today.

# 2

# The Spiritual Origins of Alcoholics Anonymous

## A Much Needed Historical Perspective

There are plenty of humble statements by Bill Wilson that he was not the originator of the ideas he wrote in A.A.'s Big Book and Twelve Steps. He often said that A.A. was not invented. He frequently added that each of A.A.'s spiritual principles was borrowed from ancient sources. Later on, he conceded that some of his text's most important ideas had come from the Oxford Group. Still later, he began telling AAs that Rev. Sam Shoemaker was the well-spring of the ideas and that almost every Step idea had come directly from the teachings of Shoemaker and from nowhere else. Shoemaker's role seemed so great that–unknown to almost any AA today–Bill had actually requested Sam Shoemaker to write the Twelve Steps. But Shoemaker had declined, suggesting they should be written by an alcoholic.

Bill's statements about borrowing principles, about the Oxford Group, and about Shoemaker were truthful as far as they went. But they went nowhere near far enough. He never mentioned the Bible. He never mentioned Anne Smith. He never mentioned the Christian literature AAs read regularly. He never discussed the extent and significance of Quiet Time. And, even as to the Oxford Group and Shoemaker, he certainly never detailed the actual words, phrases, or specific teachings he had either "borrowed" or paraphrased from these latter two sources.

Today, after sixteen years of research, I can say that we have for study most of the specifics that Wilson omitted. I got them from archives, interviews, correspondence, historians, AAs, and the study of a great many books, papers, and letters. You'll find the results in my 26 published titles and over 120 articles (See http://www.dickb.com/titles.shtml; http://www.dickb-blog.com).

I can say unequivocally that there is one major pre-requisite to reporting A.A. history. It is an implied mandate that is rarely noticed, perhaps because some might think there was, or that it might demonstrate, a rift between Bill Wilson and Dr. Bob–which there wasn't.

The point is that the reporter must recognize and report that A.A.'s "program" had two distinctly different origins and ingredients. Yet only one of these has ever really hit the pages of A.A.'s "official" literature in any significant way. In fact, practically no historians have highlighted the difference. Moreover, the second origin brings up a topic that later AAs have seemed to spend decades burying–the Christian roots of A.A.'s ideas, practices, and real successes. To get the picture, one must recognize the historical point commonly ignored concerning the "borrowing" and "fashioning" of the program by each of its co-founders Wilson and Smith.

The fact is that Bill Wilson's sources, spiritual infusions, and beliefs were completely and totally different from those from which Bob Smith drew most heavily. Each man's ideas sprang from the completely and totally different backgrounds of the two Vermont "neighbors" and A.A. co-founders.

**Bill Wilson's "Religious" Background**

Let's look at Bill Wilson's background in terms of religious affiliation and religious training, if any. First, Bill was a self-proclaimed "conservative atheist," though many AAs think he was an "agnostic." In his taped "autobiography," Bill said:

> I'd been incapable of faith and so, God's help. The more I analyzed myself, the worse I got, and my whole life had been a struggle to get to what I thought would be a better environment. Yet, out of no faith, faith had suddenly appeared [*Bill W.: My First 40 Years*, *supra*, p. 147].

Musing about his friend Ebby Thacher's attempt to offer him a religious solution to alcoholism, Wilson had these things to say:

> Ebby well knew my prejudices. He knew that my god was science [*Bill W.: My First 40 Years*, *supra*, p. 133].
>
> Up to a point Ebby had made plenty of sense. Confession and restitution might be difficult. The pace he set was certainly fast. But

how was I to swallow this garbage? I'd had one of those modern educations and had learned that man is god, the spearhead of evolution [*Bill W.: My First 40 Years*, *supra*, p. 135].

Yes, if there was any great physician that could cure the alcohol sickness, I'd better seek him now, at once. I'd better find what my friend [Ebby] had found. . . I'd better get straight over to the hospital, where Dr. Silkworth would thoroughly sober me up again. Then I could look clear-eyed at my friend's formula. Perhaps I wouldn't need an emotional conversion. After all, **a conservative atheist like me ought to be able to get on without anything like that**! [emphasis added; *Bill W.: My First 40 Years*, *supra*, p. 139].

One writer, Ernest Kurtz, concluded these things about Wilson and religion–though Kurtz provides virtually no references for us to chew on:

Of Bill's earlier exposure to religion, little is known–probably because there is little to know. Grandfather Fayette, the chief influence on the boy's life, was an Ingersoll-inclined transcendentalist. In response to his ideas, the young Bill Wilson had "left the church" at about age twelve–on a "matter of principle." Ironically, the "principle" involved concerned a required temperance pledge. . . the young Wilson had no "religion" beyond an adolescent romanticism easily congruent with both his grandfather's Vermont vagueness and his friend Mark Whalon's adoring admiration of the power of the human mind (Ernest Kurtz, *Not-God*. exp. ed. Center City, MN: Hazelden, 1991, p. 16).

If you sift through the flowery sarcasm above, you would probably still agree with Kurtz that Wilson–the avowed atheist–hardly was raised a believer or a religious man. Wilson seems never to have belonged to any church at all, at least not after he was twelve years old. He certainly did experience a conversion to Christ at Shoemaker's Calvary Rescue Mission—though unquestionably drunk when he did so. Lois Wilson correctly reports what really happened there:

Well, people got up and went to the altar and gave themselves to Christ. And the leader of the meeting asked if there was anybody that wanted to come up. And Bill started up. . . . And he went up to the front, and really, in very great sincerity, did hand over his life to Christ [For this little if ever mentioned fact of the decision for Christ that Bill made at Calvary Mission, I am indebted to A.A. historian Richard K., who obtained and supplied me with the foregoing account from the record of Lois Wilson's June 29, 1973 talk in Dallas, Texas]

Describing the earliest moments after Bill's Rescue Mission conversion, Bill told Ed B., in a recorded conversation, "For sure I was born again." I have seen the transcript, and it is also repeated in Hazelden's reprint under the title "*Bill W.: An Autobiography*. Also, in a letter to a relative that I found in the Stepping Stones archives, Bill chirped: "I've got religion"–the very thing Ebby Thacher had said to Bill when Ebby visited Bill and related his conversion at Calvary Mission.

But very soon after this Calvary Mission conversion, Bill began making no mention of his acceptance of Christ at the altar there, and he chose to ignore and virtually hide its implication. For decades, he chose to call his subsequent "conversion experience" at Towns Hospital (which occurred a few days after his acceptance of Christ at the Rescue Mission) a "spiritual experience" and later a "spiritual awakening." Not surprising that Bill switched expressions. For he had married a non-Christian (Lois Burnham Wilson), who came from a non-Christian family–Swedenborgian in membership and belief. Bill wedded Lois Burnham in the non-Christian Swedenborgian church. And Lois's comments are very illuminating about the disappearance of the "conversion" story. Note, that as for the Oxford Group's Christian fellowship and Bill W.'s conversion, Bill's wife Lois confided: "Well, I didn't have much use for the Oxford Group. I didn't think I needed 'conversion.' (See Kurtz, *supra*, p. 315, n. 58). In three words we can accurately say that: Lois Wilson was *not a believer*.

For many years after his own conversion, Wilson himself had virtually nothing to say about Jesus Christ or about early A.A.'s Christian fellowship though he did remark at Yale that "most of us were practicing Christians." Also, Dale Mitchel, who wrote the biography of Bill Wilson's physician Dr. Silkworth said:

> Several sources, including Norman Vincent Peale in his book *The Positive Power of Jesus Christ*, agree that it was Dr. Silkworth who used the term "The Great Physician" to explain the need in recovery for a relationship with Jesus Christ. If true, this reference to Jesus has all but been eliminated from the Alcoholics Anonymous History. In the formation of A.A., Wilson initially insisted on references to God and Jesus, as well as the Great Physician. As the fellowship grew, however, other members persuaded Bill that a purely Christian format would alienate many, keeping potential members away from joining the group (Mitchel, *Silkworth*, *supra*, p. 50).

Just what was Bill Wilson's position after his Rescue Mission decision for Christ, after his discussions with Dr. Silkworth about "The Great

Physician," and after he cried out for help from the Great Physician and his Heavenly Father? I don't really think we will ever find out. We'll only know a snippet here and a snippet there. We know that Bill said to A.A. Number Three and his wife (the Dotsons) that the Lord had cured him of his terrible disease and that he wanted to keep telling people about it (*Alcoholics Anonymous* 4th ed., p. 191). We know that Bill's New York friend and supporter John Henry Fitzhugh Mayo very much wanted the Big Book to retain the Christian and Bible materials of early A.A. We also know that a decision was made between Bill, Hank Parkhurst, and Fitz in the office of Bill's secretary to reject Fitz's views; and we know that some 400 pages of the original manuscript were tossed out, apparently in pursuance of that decision. Lois Wilson later claimed in her autobiography that it was agreed that A.A. should be a "universal" program because not all drunks were Christians. But Bill himself very daintily danced around his own status as a believer—spending hours and hours with Rev. Sam Shoemaker of Calvary Episcopal Church and remaining Shoemaker's life-long friend, and also spending hours and hours with the Jesuit priest Father Ed Dowling, whom he called his spiritual sponsor. So we leave it to others to discover just why Bill switched from the man who made a decision for Christ and who said the Lord had cured him to a man who stood by while Christianity was eliminated from his baby, the Big Book.

Bill stated unequivocally to T. Henry and Clarace Williams in 1954 that he had never cracked a Bible until after he met Dr. Bob in Akron. Bill's later admirers repeatedly soft-pedaled his brief early A.A. Christian leanings and beliefs, by labeling him as "spiritual, but not religious"-whatever that means to the admirers, or to you. Putting it the various pieces together, it is easy to state that Bill Wilson's Biblical and Christian background, if any, was next to nil. It is equally easy to quote Bill's statement that he was always running around "teaching spiritual kindergarten" and therefore having little of the religious background of his partner Dr. Bob.

**Dr. Bob's Bible Training, Christian Beliefs, and Religious Affiliations**

Compare the Wilson facts with those concerning Dr. Bob. Dr. Robert H. Smith had been a Christian believer from his earliest days. He belonged to a series of Protestant Christian churches most of his life–the North Congregational Church in Vermont; then, in Akron, St. Luke's; then, the Church of Our Saviour; then with his wife Anne as a charter member, the

Westside Presbyterian Church; and finally St. Paul's Protestant Episcopal Church in Akron the last year of his life.

Bob had been an avid Bible student and had received what he called "excellent training" as a youngster in Christian Endeavor. Bob married a Christian woman, Anne Ripley Smith. Bob studied the Bible extensively. He read almost every Oxford Group/Shoemaker book that was available. He devoured Christian literature of the day. He was a daily user of devotionals such as *The Upper Room*, *My Utmost for His Highest*, and *The Runner's Bible.* Bob told his son that he had probably read such materials for at least an hour a day most of his life. And Bob later circulated and recommended a multitude of Christian materials to A.A. pioneers and their families. In his own life, he usually prayed three times each day. In several different ways, Bill Wilson declared himself in awe of Dr. Bob's spiritual knowledge and studies. Bill said Dr. Bob was far ahead of him on that score. Bill added that he (Bill) had always merely been running around "teaching spiritual kindergarten."

**The Historical Void in Recognizing the Differences between A.A.'s Two Founders**

Regrettably, practically no historical work on A.A. takes account of, earmarks, analyzes, or incorporates the tremendous impact on the ultimate A.A. program that was caused by the two totally different background points from which Bill and Bob had, respectively, begun their spiritual quests. This does not mean that there were two A.A. founding factions fighting with each other; nor that there were two founders disagreeing with each other. There were simply two distinctly different points of origin of the ultimate A.A. program. In my opinion, the resultant different approaches will never be reconciled into one A.A. "program" because each founder ultimately used a different set of tools–Dr. Bob's tools having been all but buried. And forever in today's A.A. hierarchy! We have found them, but disseminating the facts within the fellowship is another story entirely.

## The Bible/Dr. Bob Source

(A.A.'s Akron Genesis springing from Dr. Bob's youth in St. Johnsbury, Vermont)

**The Akron Genesis and its Bible/Dr. Bob Source**

A.A.'s Akron Genesis began with Dr. Bob, his church activities as a youngster, and his excellent Bible and religious training in the North Congregational Church at St. Johnsbury, Vermont, where he and his parents worshiped. Also with Bob's participation in the Christian Endeavor work in those days. See Dick B., *Dr. Bob and His Library*, 3rd ed. (Kihei, HI: Paradise Research Publications, Inc., 1998; *The James Club and The Early A.A. Program's Absolute Essentials*, 4th ed, Kihei, HI: Paradise Research Publications, Inc., 2005).

**Dr. Bob's Youth, Religious Training, and Christian Church Involvement**

Dr. Bob was born and raised in St. Johnsbury, Vermont. His parents were pillars of the North Congregational Church in St. Johnsbury. From childhood through high school, Bob each week attended that Congregational church, its Sunday School, evening service, Monday night Christian Endeavor meetings, and sometimes its Wednesday evening prayer meeting. These actions were likely at the insistence of his mother. Yet, Bob continued membership in Christian churches during most of his life: St. Johnsbury Congregational in his youth. Possibly St. Luke's Protestant Episcopal Church. Probably the Church of Our Saviour in Akron, where his kids attended Sunday School. Then Akron's Westminster Presbyterian Church where Dr. Bob and his wife Anne Smith were charter members from June 3, 1936 to April 3, 1942. Finally, a year before his death, Dr. Bob became a communicant at St. Paul's Episcopal Church in Akron. This Episcopal Church was the so-called "Firestone" church of which Dr. Walter Tunks was rector—Tunks having been associated in many ways with A.A.'s Akron beginnings.

**Dr. Bob's Assertions on the Bible's Importance**

Dr. Bob specifically told AAs he had nothing to do with writing the Twelve Steps. Nor did he have much to do with the writing of A.A.'s basic text, the "Big Book," other than to review manuscripts as Bill Wilson passed them to Bob for approval prior to publication in the Spring of 1939. But Dr. Bob did make some very clear statements about the Bible and A.A. And it was from and in Akron that A.A.'s basic biblical ideas were discussed, honed, tried, and then later put into terse and tangible form and left to Bill Wilson's hands in A.A.'s "Big Book" and Twelve Steps.

Dr. Bob said A.A.'s basic ideas came from the Bible. Both Dr. Bob and Bill often stated that Jesus's sermon on the mount contained the underlying spiritual philosophy of A.A. Bob often read Bible passages in the sermon (which is found in Matthew Chapters Five, Six, and Seven). Bob specifically pointed out that the A.A. slogans "First Things First" and "Easy Does It" were taken respectively from Matthew 6:33 and 6:34. Furthermore, when someone asked Dr. Bob a question about the A.A. program, his usual response was: "What does it say in the Good Book?" He declared that A.A. pioneers were "convinced that the answer to their problems was in the Good Book." He added: "To some of us older ones, the parts we found absolutely essential were the Sermon on the Mount, the 13th chapter of First Corinthians, and the Book of James." Thus fact, James was so popular with the pioneers that, according to Bill Wilson, many favored calling the A.A. fellowship "The James Club." See *Pass It On.* (NY: Alcoholics Anonymous World Services, Inc., 1984), p. 147; and Dick B., *The James Club, supra*.

**Old Fashioned Prayer and Revival in Akron Meetings**

The Biblical emphasis in A.A.'s "Akron Group No. One" involved much much more than mentioned above or discussed in A.A.'s *DR. BOB and The Good Oldtimers*. The pioneer meetings opened with Christian prayer. As mentioned, they were "old fashioned prayer meetings." Dr. Bob's son called them "revival meetings." Bible devotionals such as *The Upper Room, My Utmost for His Highest*, and *The Runner's Bible* were regular fare. Also in individual Quiet Times, and Quiet Times with Anne Smith each morning at the Smith home. Quiet Time itself had distinct Biblical roots. See Dick B., *Good Morning!: Quiet Time, Morning Watch, Meditation, and Early A.A.*, 2d ed. (Kihei, HI: Paradise Research Publications, Inc., 1998). Scripture was regularly read at all meetings. Scripture, both from devotionals and from actual reading of the Good Book, was often the fountainhead for topics discussed at pioneer meetings. Bible study itself was stressed. Dr. Bob called every meeting of early A.A. a "Christian Fellowship;" and early A.A. was in fact an integral part of "A First Century Christian Fellowship." Also, as will be detailed later, every single Twelve Step idea can be traced to specific Bible verses and segments, whether those Bible ideas came directly from Bill and Bob's Bible discussions or from the heavy emphasis that both the Oxford Group and Rev. Sam Shoemaker placed on the Bible and the life-changing ideas derived from its verses.

Furthermore, "Surrenders" were required in early Akron A.A. In the weekly meetings on Wednesdays, there were "real surrenders." The newcomer was taken upstairs by Dr. Bob and T. Henry Williams and one or two older members. The newcomer accepted on his knees Jesus Christ as Lord and Saviour. Older members then prayed with newcomers in the manner specified in James 5:16. The men prayed with him that alcohol be taken out of his life and that he be given the strength and guidance to live by the teachings of Jesus Christ—particularly the so-called "Four Absolutes"—Honesty, Purity, Unselfishness, and Love. See Dick B., *The Good Book and The Big Book: A.A.'s Roots in the Bible*, 2d ed. (Kihei, HI: Paradise Research Publications, Inc., 1997); *The Akron Genesis of Alcoholics Anonymous, supra; DR. BOB and the Good Oldtimers, supra; That Amazing Grace: The Role of Clarence and Grace S. in Alcoholics Anonymous, supra; Cured!, supra..*

And how did all these Christian and Bible-oriented principles and practices wind up in A.A.? As mentioned above, some of the principal ones closely resembled long-standing ideas of the Christian community and of the Salvation Army. They certain did not come from, nor could properly be described as through, Bill Wilson. They were the daily grist of the Akron experimental work to deliver drunks. Program ideas with which Dr. Bob had been familiar since his Vermont days—Confession of Christ, reliance on the Creator, elimination of sin, growth in fellowship with Bible study and prayer, reading religious literature, fellowship, and witness. These were coupled with the requirements of abstinence, resisting temptation, and usually hospitalization in the earliest days of recovery..

That introduces a final point. One that really marks the beginning of the Akron Genesis. Its details were only recently unearthed in the author's research. This point has to do with Christian Endeavor, the Christian church movement for youth to which Dr. Bob belonged as a youngster. And that movement, its practices, and principles can be seen as having great impact on many of the basic and *unique* aspects of Akron A.A.. These aspects differed from the Oxford Group approaches and principles with which Bill Wilson had been indoctrinated on the East Coast. They did not involve the Four Absolutes, nor the 5 C's, nor Restitution, nor Guidance as such, nor the Surrenders, nor the house-parties, nor the teams, nor other distinctly Oxford Group ideas with which Bob and Bill were both familiar from their respective Oxford Group connections.

**The Christian Endeavor Movement Impact**

Akron A.A.'s prayer meetings, conversion meetings, Bible study meetings, devotional literature, religious discussions, confession of Christ, emphasis on church affiliation, and Christian outreach were a distinct characteristic of the Akron program. They were not emphasized in New York. They showed the influence that Christian Endeavor had exerted on Dr. Bob. See Dick B., *The Books Early AAs Read for Spiritual Growth*, 7th ed. (Kihei, HI: Paradise Research Publications, 1998), pp. 13-17; *Cured!: Proven Help for Alcoholics and Addicts* (Kihei, HI: Paradise Research Publications, Inc., 2005); *Dr. Bob and His Library*, 3rd ed. (Kihei, HI: Paradise Research Publications, Inc., 1998); Amos R. Wells, *Expert Endeavor: A Text-book of Christian Endeavor Methods and Principles* (Boston: United Society of Christian Endeavor, 1911); Francis E. Clark. *Christian Endeavor in All Lands*. (N.p.: The United Society of Christian Endeavor, 1906); *Memoirs of Many Men in Many Lands: An Autobiography* (Boston: United Society of Christian Endeavor, 1922); James DeForest Murch, *Successful C.E. Prayer-Meetings* (Cincinnati: The Standard Publishing Company, 1930).

Christian Endeavor was a movement formed in Williston Congregational Church in Portland, Maine on February 2, 1881. It was designed to meet the need of the church for training young Christians. Activities included the weekly young people's prayer meeting. Each member promised to attend and take some part. A Bible verse or a sentence of prayer answered the individual's obligation of "taking some part aside from singing." In addition to prayer meetings, there were social gatherings, missionary committees, music and floral committees, and committees to visit the sick and poor and welcome strangers. The organization endeavored to be self-governing and self-propagating. It spread to Massachusetts, Rhode Island, and Vermont. Then to numerous U.S. churches, to Hawaii, China, and many parts of the world. In a few years, nearly 25,000 young people journeyed across the United States to attend a convention in San Francisco. Ultimately, membership far exceeded three million.

**Descriptions of Christian Endeavor**

Rev. Francis E. Clark, Founder of the Christian Endeavor Movement, said the roots of the Christian Endeavor tree were: (1) Confession of Christ. (2) Service for Christ. (3) Fellowship with Christ's people. (4) And Loyalty to Christ's Church. As to the Confession of Christ, Clark said: "Confession of Christ is absolutely necessary in the Christian Endeavor Society. . . . Every week comes the prayer meeting in which every member who fulfills his vow must take some part. . . . The true Christian Endeavorer. . . .does take part to show that he is a Christian, to confess his love for the Lord. . . . The covenant pledge. . . secures familiarity with the Word of God by promoting Bible-reading and study in preparation for every meeting."

Rev. F. B. Meyer, who later was to have a substantial influence on the Oxford Group and on early A.A. ideas and was president of the British Christian Endeavor Union, said Christian Endeavor stood for five great principles: (1) Personal devotion to the divine Lord and Saviour, Jesus Christ. (2) The covenant obligation embodied in our pledge. (3) Constant religious training for all kinds of service. (4) Strenuous loyalty to the local church and denomination with which each society is connected. (5) Interdenominational spiritual fellowship.

The C.E. founder, Rev. Francis Clark, summarized the C.E. covenant as follows:

> Trusting in the Lord Jesus for strength, I promise him that I will strive to do whatever He would like to have me do; that I will pray and read the Bible every day; and that, just so far as I know how, I will endeavor to lead a Christian life. I will be present at every meeting of the society, unless prevented by some reason which I can conscientiously give to my Saviour, and will take part in the meeting, either by prayer, testimony, or a Bible verse. As an active member of this society, I promise to be faithful to my own church, and to do all I can to uphold its works and membership.

Amos R. Wells, Editorial Secretary of the United Society of Christian Endeavor, asked: (1) What are the results we may gain from the prayer meeting? They are five: original thought on religious subjects; open committal to the cause of Christ; the helpful expression of Christian thought and experience; the cultivation of the spirit of worship through public prayer and singing; the guidance of others along these lines of service and life. (2) How can we get original thought on the prayer-meeting topics? Only by study of the Bible, followed by meditation. First, the Endeavorer should read the Bible passage; then he should read some good commentary upon it; then he should take the subject with him into his daily life. (3) Are we to read Bible verses and other quotations? Yes, all we please, if we will make them the original expression of our own lives by thinking about them, and adding to them something, if only a sentence, to show that we have made them our own.

If you read A.A.'s *DR. BOB and the Good Oldtimers*, as well as my own titles on early A.A., you will see unique Christian Endeavor parallels and practices in what was called the Akron "Program." In fact, if you read the personal stories of the pioneers in the First Edition of A.A.'s Big Book, you will see the practices in action. To be sure, the Akron pioneers often called themselves the alcoholic squad of the Oxford Group (*DR. BOB and the Good Oldtimers, supra*, p. 117). They also called themselves a "Christian fellowship" (*DR. BOB, supra*, p. 118) as well as the "Alcoholic Group of Akron, Ohio" (*DR. BOB, supra*, p. 128). But their unique meeting structure was not like that of most Oxford Group meetings or "house parties." In fact, their Wednesday program was also called a "clandestine" or secret lodge of that Group (*DR. BOB, supra*, p. 121). Moreover, the Akron practices were not familiar to eastern Oxford Grouper Bill Wilson when he came to Akron. This, in part, because Akron meetings resembled Christian Endeavor meetings in a number of ways.

As stated, the Akron A.A. meetings were called "old fashioned prayer meetings" and "Christian Fellowships." Group study of the Bible, meditation. reading of Bible literature, and discussion of topics from the Bible as they impacted on the member's life all contained ingredients different from those at Sam Shoemaker's Calvary House. So too Akron's mandatory surrender to Jesus Christ. There was nothing in the Oxford Group program that bore resemblance to the Christian prayer sessions for a newcomer in the upstairs of the Williams and Smith homes. There was nothing in the Oxford Group representing the Christian Endeavor's self-support and self-propagation credo, emphasis on alignment with some church, fellowship with like-minded believers, service, and Christian witness. Nor was Oxford Group "story telling" and "news, not views" a feature of Christian Endeavor fellowships.

The unique Akron elements caused Akron's "program" to be described as first century Christianity such as that found in the Book of Acts (*DR. BOB, supra*, pp.129-31, 135-36; Nan Robertson, *Getting Better Inside Alcoholics Anonymous.* NY: Fawcett Crest, 1988, p, 54); and these elements were the heart of Akron A.A. Dr. Robert H. Smith was no Sam Shoemaker or Frank Buchman. Nan Robertson appropriately wrote:

> Beginning in 1935, Dr. Bob quickly became an extraordinarily effective worker with active alcoholics. He was tough. He was inflexible. He told his prospects: "Do you want to surrender to God? Take it or leave it." Soon, carloads of drunks were coming to Akron

> from as far away as Cleveland to meet in his house. Recently, Young Bob tried to explain why his father had been so successful at "fixing" drunks:. . . "He knew that a drunk coming out of an alcoholic haze would be absolutely overwhelmed by anything but a straightforward program that anyone could understand. It wasn't aimed at college grads–he kept it simple so that anyone was capable of grasping it." The doctor was authoritative, and he was impressive [Robertson, *Getting Better*, supra, p. 48].

Most assuredly, common spillovers from Oxford Group life-changing techniques were present in both New York and Akron A.A. beginnings. But the Oxford Group had a host of leaders, teams, authors, and writings. Akron had two: Dr. Bob and the Good Book, and the Akron Genesis was unquestionably biblical.

## The Oxford Group/Bill W. Source

(The New York Genesis: Rowland Hazard's visit to Dr. Carl Jung and Shoemaker's teachings)

There is no need here to dwell on A.A.'s New York beginnings, other than to point out that they never produced any significant results in curing drunks until long after the Akron program was developed, reported, approved, and utilized as the basis for Bill's Big Book writings.

A.A.'s New York Genesis has often been recorded, albeit grossly over-emphasized, distorted, and even mis-reported. We should and will therefore repeat some all important facts: Bill Wilson, a Brooklyn resident, was a self-proclaimed "conservative atheist"–a fact only recently coming to be accepted, largely because of my research at Stepping Stones, particularly in a so-called "Bedford Manuscript" that transcribed Bill's taped memoirs. Bill had never ever been involved in any significant way with any church, Protestant or Roman Catholic, and certainly not as a member. Moreover, by his own statement, Bill had never, until he came to Akron in 1935, "looked in the Bible, up to this time, at all. You see, [said Bill] I had the [conversion] experience first and then this rushing around to help drunks and nothing happened." See Dick B., *The Akron Genesis of Alcoholics Anonymous*, 2d ed. (Kihei, HI: Paradise Research Publications), 1998, p. 64.

**The Rowland Hazard Starting Point for the New York Genesis**

An East Coast businessman named Rowland Hazard sought help for his alcoholism from the famed psychiatrist, Dr. Carl Gustav Jung, in Switzerland. Hazard's treatment was followed by return to drinking. When Hazard went back to Jung for more help, Jung told him he had the mind of a chronic alcoholic and would need a conversion to overcome his compulsion. Jung defined such a conversion as "union with God." He suggested that Rowland seek this experience in a religious association.

Rowland therefore joined "A First Century Christian Fellowship," also then known as the "Oxford Group." Rowland followed its precepts. I have never seen any indication from his remarks or writings that indicated he had a "spiritual experience." He simply was cured of alcoholism, and helped rescue a New Yorker named Ebby Thacher from incarceration for chronic drunkenness. In so doing, Rowland had indoctrinated Ebby with the Oxford Group's life-changing ideas and lodged Ebby in Calvary Rescue Mission, which was part of Rev. Sam Shoemaker's Calvary Episcopal Church in New York. There Ebby became a born again Christian—making a decision for Christ at the Mission altar. He also desired to witness to others–particularly to his old drinking buddy Bill Wilson. Accordingly, Ebby visited and convinced his suffering friend Bill Wilson that he (Ebby) had "got religion," had been to Shoemaker's Rescue Mission, and that "God had done for him what he could not do for himself."

**Wilson's Conversions**

Though drunk while on his way, Wilson marched to the Rescue Mission, announced he wanted what Ebby had received, responded to an altar call, and [according to Mrs. Samuel Shoemaker who was there and related the facts to me in a phone conversation I had with her personally.] made his decision for Christ. As related above, I only recently discovered that Lois Wilson had explicitly told of Bill's giving his life to Christ at Calvary. In a little or never mentioned writing, Bill echoed Ebby's Oxford Group words, saying "I've got religion." He related that "for sure he was born again." Bill truly believed he had really "found something" and, after more drinking, checked into Towns Hospital in New York–where he had been hospitalized before in the care of Dr. William Silkworth. During his hospital stay, Bill again heard some key Oxford Group principles in visits to him by Ebby Thacher. Bill also then had what he frequently was to call his "hot flash" conversion experience. He validated it by talking it over with Silkworth and by reading William James' book on *Varieties of Religious Experience*.

Unlike Ebby, Bill was not successful in witnessing to others. For upon his release from Towns Hospital, Bill did not succeed in "converting" anyone to the Oxford Group life-change. Nor did he succeed in getting one single drunk sober during the period he was bringing drunks to his Brooklyn home for help. Nor, it is quite clear, did he really succeed in getting more than one or two drunks cured in the New York area for quite some time. Some have claimed this was because Bill was "preaching" to the unfortunates. However, I am convinced that **Bill was a "preacher" without a sermon.** A messenger without the true message. He really had no significant Oxford Group training in those early days. He had no Bible training at all. He had no church teaching to draw on. And, not surprisingly, he had no message to carry that had the kind of impact which became commonplace in Akron later on.

But that's not the way most historians have told it. According to the regular packaged stories: 1) Bill was "preaching;" 2) Bill was failing because of his preaching; and 3) Bill was told by Dr. Silkworth to hit his newcomers with the deadly facts about alcoholism first, and then to give them the Oxford Group message. But **it still did not work!** I submit, however, that it could hardly work when the "preacher" had been converted while drunk, when the "preacher" had never studied the Bible at all, and when his whole starting point was that of a hesitant atheist who never went on to study the Word, read religious literature, or join a church.

### The Real Message as to a New Man in Christ Was Yet to Be Fashioned–and Not by Bill

In New York, Bill had obviously assimilated some major Oxford Group life-changing ideas before he met Dr. Bob in Akron in May of 1935. Seemingly, as early as the beginning of his sobriety in late 1934. Bill could not have gotten within hearing distance of the dynamic life-changer, Rev. Sam Shoemaker, without hearing the real message Sam consistently preached. It is expressed as follows in Sam's very first title–widely read by Oxford Group people even to this day. In *Realizing Religion* (NY: The Association Press, 1921), Sam had written of his own quest:

> . . . [T]he first stage of the development. . . was this: a superb and conquering self-assurance, melting under a growing spiritual aspiration into conscious inadequacy, the increasing sense of sin and later the

serpent putting up his head for one final attack, a deep hunger for rebirth, the actual discovery of Christ in conversion, and the search for means to keep this experience alive (p. viii).

Now the thing which is striking about much of the misery one sees is that it is spiritual misery. It is the unhappiness of spiritual people very often–souls who are too fine-grained to get along without religion, yet who have never come to terms with it. It is the sadness of maladjustment to the eternal things, and this throws out the whole focus of life. Rest cures and exercise and motor drives will not help. The only thing that will help is religion. For the root of the malady is estrangement from God–estrangement from Him in people that were made to be His companions (pp. 4-5).

Something is lacking. Somehow we have missed the way. Yes, life is complex–but we know that if our souls were simpler our lives would be better ordered. . . most of all, we are "dissatisfied with ourselves." . . . All of us cling, despite all proofs to the contrary, to the idea that we are different, and need something that others do not need, and never can be satisfied with any generally accepted idea about religion. But this is our old pride raising its head for a last thrust. Our heavenly Father knows where we are really different. What you want is simply a vital religious experience. You need to find God. You need Jesus Christ (pp. 8-9).

Christianity means only one thing: it means relationship with Christ. . . . What does it mean to accept Christ? Nothing humiliating, or superstitious, or irrational. You allow Him to set in motion a relationship between you. You enter upon a new companionship. . . . If there are theological problems which hinder, clear them up as you can, remembering always their relatively inferior importance to the "reality of the relation to Christ." Take as much as you can, and work for more (pp. 42-43).

Many Akron Pioneers, and many Oxford Group people frequently quoted 2 Corinthians 5:17. That verse spoke to the result of following the path to God through Christ:

2 Cor. 5:17:
Therefore if any man *be* in Christ, *he is* a new creature: old things are passed away; behold, all things are become new.

This verse must have seemed strange to Bill Wilson. He somehow felt that God would, if asked, "remove" the old man ideas that beset the alcoholic mind and, for that matter, the minds of all who walked by the flesh rather than the spirit. Somehow, Bill seemed never to have understood or accepted the idea that Christians *are victorious.* They *are* victorious. Victorious, not because of works, but because of what Christ accomplished for them. Bill gave no evidence of believing the following in the Book of Ephesians:

> Eph. 2:4-9:
> But God, who is rich in mercy, for his great love wherewith he loved us, Even when we were dead in sins, hath quickened *us* together with Christ (by grace ye are saved;) And hath raised *us* up together, and made *us* sit together in heavenly *places* in Christ Jesus: That in the ages to come he might shew the exceeding riches of his grace in *his* kindness toward us through Christ Jesus. For by grace are ye saved through faith; and that not of yourselves: *it is* the gift of God: Not of works, lest any man should boast.

Certainly, Sam Shoemaker knew and taught these ideas. Here are some Shoemaker examples that Bill simply must have heard from Shoemaker between 1934 and Bill's completion of the Big Book in 1939:

> The chief element in the "good life" is not character, but faith–not human kindness, but the help of God. So we are converted, not only from the grip of our "sins," and not only from that thralldom to self and time and this world which is the essence of paganism, but from all efforts to be good "on our own." To whom are we converted? Not to a set of vague ideals. Not to a humanly conceived "good life." Not to our own "better selves." We are converted, as Christians, to Jesus. . . . We become converted to Him when we accept Him in all His regal claims, saying often on our way perhaps, "Lord, I believe; help thou mine unbelief," but coming back to Him again and again, each time with more conviction about who He is. We are converted when we make an act of faith which accepts Him on His own terms, and surrender ourselves to Him, abandoning our sins so far as we can, and letting His life pour into us and through us [Shoemaker, *Extraordinary Living, supra*, pp. 128-29].

Shoemaker was teaching that believers become complete–not because of what they do and have done–but because of what the Son of God made available to them by his crucifixion, death, resurrection, ascension, and petition to his Father. Akron A.A. pioneers insisted that alcoholic newcomers accept Christ and become new persons with the power of God that comes to believers (Acts 1:1-8). Then they were to walk in the truth of God's Word. These newcomers were, of course, to seek what was "good" by God's standards; but they were to achieve those standards not alone "works" but rather with the power of God which "poured into them with the gift of the Holy Spirit," as Sam Shoemaker had expressed it. Thus Shoemaker had taught:

> God bless us and make us discontent with standing anywhere but in the midst of the full flow of His grace and power, and with doing anything less than loosing that blessed power upon the sick and fearful and unreached and bewildered and seeking folk of our time, who will never in all their lives be satisfied till they find Christ, and through Him find the Holy Spirit, and through Him find the power which it is His alone to give. "Ye shall have power, after that the Holy Ghost is come upon you" [Shoemaker, *Extraordinary Living*, *supra*, p. 143; and Acts 1:1-8].

The Bible was speaking of the gift of God that saved believers and gave them power over sin. Shoemaker was speaking of the grace–not actions–that God gave to His children. Wilson never seemed to go much farther with that than quoting the Book of James: "faith without works is dead."

And that didn't cut it. Take away the Bible. Take away Jesus Christ. Take away the gift of God; and about all you do have is "works."

The difference between Akron A.A. and New York A.A. was Christ. At the beginning, and between, it was the believers of Akron that needed to be contrasted with the unbelief that became the norm in New York. Shoemaker was a Bible Christian whose teachings were music to the ears of Dr. Bob, Anne Smith, Henrietta Seiberling, and Mr. And Mrs. T. Henry Williams. All were very conversant with Shoemaker's books and writings. But messages as to the availability of grace, salvation, and the mind of Christ presented a strange, and soon an unacceptable Christian package for Bill and Lois Wilson. Yes, they bought the sugar-coated cover up by the Emmet Fox message to A.A. people and others that the Bible has no plan of salvation and that salvation itself is a myth. Just good behavior, taught Fox. Just do the right and loving thing, Fox seemed to teach. And Shoemaker's supporter and admirer Mrs. W. Irving Harris said to me on the phone that Shoemaker and his group were "not even sure Fox was a Christian." Small wonder! Good behavior and any resultant reward don't hold a candle to the power of God in Christ in you available to all who believe. See:

2 Cor. 5:18, 19:

> And all things *are* of God, who hath reconciled us to himself by Jesus Christ, and hath given to us the ministry of reconciliation; To wit, that God was in Christ, reconciling the world unto himself, not imputing their trespasses unto them; and hath committed unto us the word of reconciliation.
>
> Eph. 1:19:
> And what is the exceeding greatness of his power to us-ward who believe, according to the working of his mighty power (Ephesians 1:19)
>
> Col. 1:26, 27:
> *Even* the mystery which hath been hid from ages and from generations, but now is made manifest to his saints. To whom God would make known what *is* the riches of the glory of this mystery among the Gentiles; which is Christ in you, the hope of glory.

God in Christ in you! A new source of power, love, and forgiveness available to those born again of the spirit. Truly a concept new to the Wilsons, appealing to the Akron pioneers, familiar to Dr. Bob and his wife Anne, and offering healing, deliverance, and forgiveness to those who wanted it. The product of what Jesus Christ accomplished:

> 1 Pet. 2:24:
> Who his own self bare our sins in his own body on the tree, that we, being dead to sins, should live unto righteousness: by whose stripes ye were healed.

Yet the New York crowd eliminated God in favor of some "higher power." They eliminated the Bible in favor of the Big Book. They tossed out Jesus Christ in favor of going to meetings. When this self-made religion began developing, a huge gap was created in the opportunity early A.A. presented for cure of alcoholism by reliance on the Creator and coming to Him through His son Jesus Christ.

Bill had certainly assimilated some major Oxford Group principles. Principles of works and good behavior. They were splattered throughout his ultimate Big Book text. These included the Five C's, the Four Absolutes, Surrender, Restitution, Guidance, Loyalty, Fellowship, and Witness. In all there were some twenty-eight Oxford Group ideas that were involved in changing lives. They definitely impacted on Bill's idea that a "spiritual" or "conversion" experience could somehow result from their practice. See Dick B., *The Oxford Group and Alcoholics*

*Anonymous: A Design for Living That Works*, 2d ed. (Kihei, HI: Paradise Research Publications,1998).

Bill endeavored to carry to drunks his version of the Oxford recovery message–probably sans the Bible and Jesus Christ. Not one drunk recovered. Not during Bill's first six months of sobriety, nor for several years as to those Bill and Lois took into their home. But in 1935, Bill carried his limited version to Dr. Bob in Akron, Ohio. There, an entirely different chain of events had been in progress. See Dick B., *The Akron Genesis of Alcoholics Anonymous*, 2d ed. (Kihei, HI: Paradise Research Publications, 1998).

## Melding the Two Different Sources Was the Appointed Task of Bill W.

Sad though it is to tell, there was a world of difference between the program of cure that *was to have been reported* by Bill, and the universalized and watered-down program *that was actually fashioned* by Bill W., the self-designated reporter. Bill had apparently visualized a world-wide outreach almost the moment he had his "hot flash" at Towns Hospital in 1934. This was a New Age one-church, one-world piece of thinking at a point where those ideas were not even yet in full flower among the flower children. However, he did not succeed with even his own outreach.

It was for Akron to achieve the successes; and when it did, Bill proposed to Dr. Bob and the pioneers that a book be written to tell how it [the Akron program] had worked. Dr. Bob was supportive, though a substantial controversy was involved. Bill obtained a split vote from the Akronites that authorized him to write a basic text describing the practices and program that the pioneers had developed to achieve their astonishing successes–which were said to amount to 75%.

As you will see in a moment, Bill's Big Book text, in its final form, did not at all report the program that had succeeded in Akron. Bill took some simple medical facts about alcoholism and the alcoholic that he had learned from his own physician Dr. William D. Silkworth. He included some substantial practical treatment ideas–probably from Richard R. Peabody's book, *The Common Sense of Drinking* (Atlantic Monthly Press Book, 1933)–copies of which were owned by both Dr. Bob and Bill.

As he dove into the program of recovery, however, Bill mentioned by name neither the Bible nor Jesus Christ as to healing or cure. He adopted some general ideas from the Akron "surrenders" but used Shoemaker terminology about "finding God" and "the turning point." The latter was a "New Thought" expression that seems to have its origin in the writings of William James. From the Oxford Group, Wilson virtually codified the Oxford Group life-changing techniques. To this mix, Bill added (using Oxford Group terms like "spiritual experience" and "spiritual awakening") Bill's own "religious experience."--all supposedly emanating from Dr. Carl Jung's prescription of a needed "conversion" for Rowland Hazard. However, Wilson's version was given a new, non-Christian, non-Biblical interpretation–both as to what constituted a "hot flash" and what constituted "finding" or "rediscovering" or "establishing a relationship" with God. To the mix were added a smattering of new thought expressions like "fourth dimension," "cosmic," "Universal Mind," and so on.

There was no mention of the necessity for being born again (John 3:1-8), being saved (John 3:16), or how to be saved (Romans 10:9). Yet all these were major items even in Oxford Group and Shoemaker teachings–albeit altered to make them palatable to Buchman's audience. They certainly were basic ideas and requirements for the Akron cures. There also was no mention of the cure the founders had sought and received and which is such an important factor in the Bible's healing accounts.

Unfortunately, Bill left to others–if anyone–the unearthing of his sources and details. And the digging–certainly mine–goes on to this very day. For some of the findings, see Dick B., *Dr. Bob and His Library*; *Good Morning: Quiet Time, Morning Watch, Meditation and Early A.A.; The Good Book and The Big Book*, *Anne Smith's Journal*; *The Akron Genesis of Alcoholics Anonymous*; *New Light on Alcoholism*; *Turning Point*; *The Oxford Group and Alcoholics Anonymous*; *God and Alcoholism; The Golden Text of A.A.; The James Club; Twelve Steps for You; Cured; Henrietta Seiberling—Ohio's Lady with a Cause;* and *By the Power of God.*

# 3

# The Akron Crucible Where It All Began

(The Place Where the Cure for the "First Forty" Was Developed between 1935 and 1938)

## The Real Program of Early A.A.

Most facets of early A.A.'s program have received little or no attention either from present-day A.A. literature, from historical accounts, or from A.A. groups themselves.

This account will put the picture on record. First, it will present a brief overview of exactly what the pioneers did while they were fashioning their program in Akron between June 10, 1935 and the publication of A.A.'s Big Book in the Spring of 1939. Second, we'll see exactly how that program was summarized after an independent and objective survey by Frank Amos in 1938–a survey whose findings were embodied in reports Amos delivered to John D. Rockefeller, Jr., in response to Rockefeller's request for information about the newly discovered cure. Third, we will look at the special role that three women pioneers played in the development stages of the program. Fourth, we will refer the reader to an excellent new booklet prepared by Richard K. on the "First Forty"–the group of about 40 pioneers whose successes caused A.A. to want to tell its story to the world. Finally we will present a unique feature of my own sixteen years of research–the actual roots of the pioneer program.

## An Overview of What They Did in Akron

**Hospitalization for about seven days**: Hospitalization and/or medical help for a brief period was virtually a "must" for most early A.A. members. During that period, only a Bible was allowed in the hospital room; medications were administered; there were daily visits and lengthy talks by Dr. Bob with the patients; there were visits by the recovered pioneers who told of their victories; there was an admission of belief in the Creator, a "surrender" to Christ, a prayer; and then release.

**Recovery in the homes**: Recovery work in Akron did not take place in groups or meetings or treatment centers; nor in rehabs or therapy or confinement. It took place primarily in homes. You might appropriately call these homes the first half-way houses, and that in itself constituted a very different situation than the one found in the Oxford Group as such. In the homes, there were (1) Daily get-togethers. (2) Bible studies and reading. (3) Individual quiet times. (4) Quiet time meetings in the Smith home in the morning with Dr. Bob's wife Anne. (5) Discussions with Dr. Bob, Henrietta Seiberling, and Anne Smith. (6) A regular Wednesday meeting with "Real" surrenders upstairs after the manner of James 5:15-16 with "elders" and prayer, acceptance of Jesus Christ, asking God to take alcohol out of their lives, and asking Him to help them live by the Four Absolutes. (7) Utilization of some Oxford Group techniques such as Inventory, Confession, Conviction, and Restitution. (8) Arranging visits to newcomers at the hospital. (9) Recommended church attendance for most. (10) Social, religious, and family fellowship.

**The Regular Wednesday Meeting**: There were no significant Oxford Group testimonials or alcoholic drunkalogs. No story-telling per se. There was a set-up meeting on Mondays where leaders sought God's guidance as to topics and leaders for the Wednesday meeting. The regular meeting involved an opening prayer; reading of Scripture; group prayer and seeking of guidance; discussion led by someone such as Dr. Bob, Henrietta Seiberling, or T. Henry Williams; "real" surrenders upstairs for the newcomers; arranging visits to the hospital; closing with the Lord's Prayer; socializing; and the exchange of Christian literature. No drunkalogs. No Steps. No Big Book. No texts at all. Just the Bible and devotionals like *The Upper Room.*

**Quiet Times:** (held by individuals, by the group, and by the morning quiet times with Anne Smith). The first condition of receiving revelation is *not* "listening" to God. It is becoming a child of God by accepting Jesus Christ as Lord and Savior. That distinction was missed entirely by someone who tried to equate "Oxford Group quiet times and two-way prayer" with the revelation available only to those who have been saved. Thus in Wally Paton's *How to Listen to God.* AZ Faith With Works Publishing Company, 2000, the author attempts to reconstruct "two-way prayer" *without Christ*. I'd call it "Christless" two-way prayer. The author goes into great length to tell the story of his own Oxford Group mentor Jim Houck (whom I know quite well).

Wally lays out the alleged Oxford Group procedures he heard from Houck. But he ignores two important things that Houck said and was quoted by Paton as saying: (1) "I met the Oxford Group on December 12, 1934 in the very same room at the Frederick, Maryland YMCA where I made a decision for Christ some sixteen years before. In 1918, I attended a church revival there. The preacher gave a sermon followed by an altar call" (Paton, *How to Listen to God*, *supra,* p.8). In other words, James Houck became a born again Christian in 1918, was "saved," and had made his decision for Christ more than a decade before he joined the Oxford Group, got sober, and later met Bill Wilson. (2) About the Oxford Group founder Frank Buchman's own attitude on conversion, Jim said:

> Frank's main objective was life-changing. He wasn't concerned so much with saving souls as he was with changing lives. Frank worked within all the churches. He didn't profess any specific beliefs, but rather, he built a program based upon a few universal truths that were an integral part of most religions. . . . He was not interested in converting people as such (Paton, *How to Listen to God*, *supra*, pp. 19, 90).

Unfortunately, Paton ignored Houck's own credentials as a born-again Christian. He then championed a "sanitized" Oxford Group quiet time (a "Christless" meditation), and seemed unaware of such "Christ-centered" writings as those by Oxford Group writer Victor Kitchen (a friend of Bill W.). In my copy of Kitchen's book–an Oxford Group best-seller–released in 1934 about the time of A.A.'s founding, Kitchen wrote, as to his own Oxford Group experience (See Victor C. Kitchen, *I Was a Pagan*. NY: Harper & Brothers, 1934):

> (1) "We were reborn into life and began, for the first time, to live under the laws of obedience" (p. 68); (2) "I see now, in other words, that to prepare us for the coming of the Holy Spirit and to direct us in the use of that unfamiliar power, God had to walk and talk among us through His Son Jesus Christ" (p. 79); (3) "They have shown me that I myself must be born in Christ and must grow in this new domain before I can assist such births and aid such growth among the members of any church congregation" (p. 150); (4) "What had I done to make myself a blood brother of Christ? I had brought Him my soiled life and He had cleansed it" (p. 176); (5) "My thanks to the Oxford Group who led me to Christ, and to Christ Who is leading me to God" (p. 186).

Incidentally, my own copy of Kitchen's book is inscribed by "Jim Houck" in his own hand. Unfortunately Paton extracted from Houck's teachings only the circumstances under which one "listened" but not the status that one must have to "hear"–a status that Houck and Kitchen each had. It was the status of sons of God, namely, that of having first been born again of God's spirit with Christ in them–the gift of the Holy Spirit.

That is certainly not to say that the Oxford Group activists all sought to be, or claimed to be, even qualified as, born again Christians. Some disdained even the use of the word "conversion" and adopted "changed" as the symbol of what they sought and received. And, concerning the "Voice" which they claimed to be able to hear, as one of their harsh critics Dr. Hensley Henson, Bishop of Durham, said: "We may also wonder whether. . . members of MRA have sufficient means for distinguishing between the genuine guidance of the Holy Spirit and the deliverances of their own sub-conscious minds masquerading as God's voice" (See Tom Driberg. *The Mystery of Moral Re-Armament*. NY: Alfred A. Knopf, 1965, pp. 192-199).

Why all this discussion of Paton, Houck, and Oxford Group guidance? There's a reason. It has to do with Jesus Christ. And I state this because of my own wide investigation of the Oxford Group. For I have personally met and known many of the early Oxford Group activists. Most were Christians, but I cannot speak for the rest. I have spoken to Jim Houck several times about his own status as a Christian and Bible student and found him to be very forthright about his acceptance of Christ and his frequent study of the Bible. But that does not mean that a present-day A.A., who applies what Paton calls the supposed (but non-existent) "Four Steps" of the Oxford Group–without first accepting Christ, as Jim Houck did, can claim to be a Christian, or an Oxford Group adherent, or even one who can "listen to God." The Oxford Group had no steps–not four, not six, and not twelve. Confessing Jesus as Lord and believing that God raised Him from the dead–a prerequisite for becoming born again–simply was not a prerequisite for either an Oxford Group "surrender to God" or a "taking" the Big Book Third and Seventh Steps. You won't find that requirement unless you talk to an Oxford Grouper like Jim Houck who had already become a born-again Christian before he entered either the Oxford Group or A.A.

The new birth, however, was a vital part of the Akron program–evidenced by the "surrender" at the hospital and often the "real surrender" in the homes. New members were required to accept Christ before they could be called members of the Akron "Christian Fellowship." Then, for born-again believers, Quiet Time consisted of reading the Bible, prayer to and seeking guidance from God, use of devotionals like *The Upper Room*, utilizing Anne Smith's Journal for teaching and instruction, and reading Christian literature such as Henry Drummond's *The Greatest Thing in the World* for greater understanding of various portions of the Bible. In fact, research has shown that the Quiet Hour–an important ingredient of United Christian Endeavor principles and practices–was something Dr. Bob had learned in, practiced during, and easily been able to apply since his days of vigorous participation in Christian Endeavor at St. Johnsbury, Vermont. And, for a general starting point as to the revelation available, at God's option, to believers, see 1 Corinthians, Chapter Twelve.

**The Emphasis of Bob and Bill together**: I have several times quoted or summarized the statements of Bob and Bill together on the platform of the Shrine Auditorium in Los Angeles in 1943. The remarks were reported in the March, 1943 issue of *The Tidings*. About 4500 AAs and their families were present. Bill spoke about the importance of Divine Aid, the religious element in A.A., and prayer. Dr. Bob spoke about the importance of cultivating the habit of prayer and reading the Bible. Both men were warmly received–a testimony to their harmonious accord, consistency, and simplicity of presentation when appearing together.

## The Frank Amos Reports in 1938

Speaking of the alcoholics in Akron, Frank Amos reported to John D. Rockefeller, Jr.: "All considered practically incurable by physicians." Yet, said Amos, they had "been reformed and so far have remained teetotalers." Their stories, he said, were remarkably alike in "the technique used and the system followed." The Amos report therefore is critically important in understanding the commonality of what they did in Akron. He described their seven-point "Program" as follows:

[**Abstinence**] An alcoholic must realize that he is an alcoholic, incurable from a medical viewpoint, and that he must never again drink anything with alcohol in it.

[**Absolute reliance on the Creator**] He must surrender himself absolutely to God, realizing that in himself there is no hope.

[**Removal of sins from his life**] Not only must he want to stop drinking permanently, he must remove from his life other sins such as hatred, adultery, and others which frequently accompany alcoholism. Unless he will do this absolutely, Smith and his associates refuse to work with him.

[**Daily Quiet Time with Bible study and prayer**] He must have devotions every morning–a "quiet time" of prayer and some reading from the Bible and other religious literature. Unless this is faithfully followed, there is grave danger of backsliding.

[**Helping other alcoholics**] He must be willing to help other alcoholics get straightened out. This throws up a protective barrier and strengthens his own willpower and convictions.

[**Fellowship**] It is important, but not vital, that he meet frequently with other reformed alcoholics and form both a social and religious comradeship.

[**Religious affiliation**] Important, but not vital, that he attend some religious service at least once weekly.

For more on the Amos investigation and reports, see *DR. BOB and the Good Oldtimers* (NY: Alcoholics Anonymous World Services), p. 131; Dick B., *God and Alcoholism: Our Growing Opportunity in the 21st Century* (Kihei, HI: Paradise Research Publications, 2002); Dick B., *The James Club and The Original A.A. Program's Absolute Essentials, 4th ed.* (Kihei, HI: Paradise Research Publications, Inc., 2005).

## The Big Book Publication in 1939

By a very slender margin, A.A. pioneers voted in Akron to let Bill Wilson write a book about how their program worked. This he began to do in 1938 and completed in the Spring of 1939.

Plenty has been said about how the Big Book was written. However, much of the story has yet to be told, and it will not be told here. Suffice it to say that Dr. Bob declared quite clearly that he did not write the Twelve Steps and had nothing to do with the writing of them. Though Wilson submitted drafts of the Big Book to Dr. Bob, very few in Akron reviewed them; and practically no changes were proposed by the Akron pioneers. Wilson, however, made very substantial changes which inserted "Power" and "higher power" and some New Thought descriptions of this mystical "Czar of the Universe." He added New Thought expressions like "fourth dimension." He eliminated all specific references to the Bible, all specific reference to fundamental Oxford Group ideas such as the Four Absolutes, the Five C's, and Jesus Christ. He made reference to supposed six word-of- mouth "steps" that he said were used in the formative years. But he described them in many different ways at varying times. Comments about a "flying blind" period began to be cast at Akron's work. And ultimately, Wilson fashioned Twelve Steps which he said *were* the Steps the A.A. new people *had taken* to find God, establish a relationship with Him, and have a "spiritual experience" that would give them a "daily reprieve" from their alcoholism.

Most of us A.A. members believe, today, that we are "taking" steps that were taken by early A.A. people. And, of course, *we are not.* We may eventually come to realize that fact. Why? First, Bill had been commissioned to write a book about how the *Akron experiment had worked.* He did not. Second, there were no Steps when Bill wrote his Big Book. The Oxford Group had no Steps whatever–not four (as one writer contends), not six (as Bill sometime contended), and certainly not Twelve. Nor did A.A. have any Steps at all. Dr. Bob said so, and that's good enough for me. Further, you'll find no mention of steps in the stories that accompanied the First Edition that was published. Bill basically fashioned his own text. He utilized the Oxford Group principles for the heart of his own program of recovery. And he added chapters for agnostics, wives, employers, families, and so on.

All the early references to "cure," to "reformed alcoholic," and to "sin"–which were stock in trade in early A.A. language and life–were discarded. See Richard K., *New Freedom: Reclaiming Alcoholics Anonymous,* 2005. Special attention was given to "agnostics" with a formula for them to choose their "own conception of God."

It goes without saying that the Wilson text book was totally different from the simple program pursued in Akron, described by Frank Amos, and productive of the 75% rate. What Wilson did do is incorporate into his Big Book most of the words, phrases, and practices of the Oxford Group and Sam Shoemaker though there is little acknowledgment of this fact in the Big Book. For the striking resemblances of Big Book language to the language of Shoemaker and the Oxford Group writings, see the following titles by Dick B., *New Light on Alcoholism*; *The Oxford Group and Alcoholics Anonymous*; *Turning Point*; *Twelve Steps for You*; *Anne Smith's Journal*; *Good Morning*; and *By the Power of God*.

## The Akron A.A. Recovery Pamphlets

I have not personally explored, documented, or verified with any of the early A.A. survivors such as Dr. Bob's children, the three Seiberling children, or even Bill Wilson's secretary Nell Wing, the following information. Nor have I verified the facts with the Akron Intergroup Archivist or the archivist at Dr. Bob's Home in Akron.

However, one writer, Wally P., claims to have searched high and low in Akron for records of the first group. He said he came away empty handed. He said he was told that the Intergroup archivist said she only had records for December 1953 and January-April, 1954 and that there was nothing prior to December 1953 or between April 1954 and April 1955. Wally wrote: "The fact that Akron, the Birthplace of A.A., is without written documentation on its first fourteen years of existence is a tragedy." See Wally P., *But, For the Grace of God. . .* Wheeling, WV: The Bishop of Books, 1995, p. 33. He added that A.A.'s New York GSO Archivist did provide some material from the 1940's, which Wally said he reviewed over the telephone, but found very little that pertained to the Akron Central Committee.

This kind of selective historical "research" explains why so much historical distortion has occurred among those who merely look for what they want instead of what there is.

Let's start with the truth: *Of course, there is written documentation! And there was when Wally was making the rounds of Intergroups.*

My twenty-six published titles are full of that documentation–from A.A.'s Akron beginnings in 1931 to Dr. Bob's death at the end of the 1940's. I will not bother here to summarize the documentation because it is the subject of my sixteen years of research and writing. I will add that Wally P. should have examined and analyzed the Akron newspaper accounts for the 1930's, Anne Smith's Journal, the Frank Amos reports, the Bill Wilson tapes of old timers (located at A.A. General Service Archives), those books in Dr. Bob's library which he obtained from Dr. Bob's daughter, the letters and messages of Henrietta Seiberling, the records of T. Henry and Clarace Williams, the archives at Dr. Bob's Home, the Founders Day archives in Akron, and hundreds of other items which were utterly ignored until after my books began to be distributed. And they are still ignored by A.A. conference approved books. In fact, almost all of the documentary 23,900 items are now lodged at Bill Wilson's birthplace in

East Dorset, Vermont, at the Griffith Library there, adjacent to the Wilson Houses.

Nonetheless, I continue with what Wally P. *did* find and which can also be found by anyone who contacts the Akron Intergroup Office and asks for it. There are five pamphlets which cover every aspect of the program as pioneers apparently saw it in the period before Dr. Bob's death. These pamphlets are: *A Manual for Alcoholics*, *A Guide to the Twelve Steps*, *Spiritual Milestones in A.A.*, and *Second Reader in A.A.*, plus the *Four Absolutes.* I've discussed the contents of these informative pamphlets in many of my titles, particularly *The Good Book and The Big Book*, *The Akron Genesis of Alcoholics Anonymous*, and *Turning Point*. According to Wally P., one of the pamphlets says this on its cover:

> This pamphlet was written and edited by members of Alcoholics Anonymous of Akron, Ohio. It was in Akron that Alcoholics Anonymous was founded. Among Akron members are one of the founders, the first person to accept the program, and a large number of other members whose sobriety dates back to 1935, 1936 , and 1937 [Wally P., *But for the Grace of God...*, *supra*, p. 37].

The same writer claims to have learned the following from Akron's Intergroup Archivist: She who had a telephone interview with the son of Evan W.–who wrote the pamphlets and who told the archivist by telephone:

> Evan W. had been an editor of the Akron Beacon Journal, but he had been fired because of his alcoholism. He was later rehired at an entry level position. He got sober in May, 1941. Once Evan was on his feet, Dr. Bob asked him to write some "Blue Collar A.A." pamphlets for the fellowship. As Dr. Bob explained, the Big Book was too complicated for many A.A.'s and he wanted Evan to present the program in its most basic terms [Wally P., *But for the Grace of God*, *supra*, p. 42].

Such tidbits don't meet the test of "evidence." They are hearsay on hearsay on hearsay, but we're not in a courtroom. They are very useful. The pamphlets do exist in revised form today. They can be purchased from the Akron Intergroup office. They do speak of a program that does not remotely resemble the program that Wilson set forth in his Big Book. And they are Biblical from start to finish. No historian should purport to set out A.A. history without dealing with these Akron pamphlets, the mounds and mounds of evidence from Akron, the Frank Amos reports, and Anne Smith's Journal–which records what was done and by an eyewitness who did it!

## The Special Role of Three Women Pioneers

Please note that the contents of this portion were addressed in more detail by Veronica R., a woman speaker and teacher from Woodland, California. She covered them in her address at The Second Nationwide Alcoholics Anonymous History Conference in Wilmington, Delaware, on August 22-23, 2003. My own coverage of the points can be found in materials I have written before.

### Anne Ripley Smith, "Mother of A.A.," Wife of Dr. Bob

It should never have been, and should not be, necessary to write the details about the most forgotten and most frequently unmentioned (yet one of the most influential) founders of Alcoholics Anonymous. Yet you will not find her even mentioned in Bill Wilson's Big Book text–though Wilson actually asked her to write its chapter "To Wives" (which she diplomatically declined to do). When she died, Bill Wilson solicited letters about her yet never fulfilled his promise to publish them in A.A. literature. When an A.A. staff member was dispatched from New York to gather material for and write *DR. BOB and the Good Oldtimers* (the intended biography of Dr. Bob and the Akron pioneers), the staff member was asked by Dr. Bob's son if he was going to write about Dr. Bob's wife (Anne). And the staffer said, "No!" Finally after remonstrances from Dr. Bob's two children–whom he was interviewing–he agreed to write about Anne in the Akron biography. However, a moment's glance at that book will show how inadequately her historical role was covered. Her vitally informative journal is unmentioned.

The pity is that nothing significant–other than my own work on Anne Ripley Smith–has ever been published by A.A. or anyone else about Anne Smith's Journal. Despite the fact that the journal tells the story of what early A.A. pioneers studied and heard. Nor, for that matter, has anything significant been written about Anne herself–as far as her enormous work and sacrifice in the early A.A. program. Anne's 64 page hand-written work actually recorded what was going on and being discussed in A.A. and by its forbears from 1933 to 1939. Recently, I read a good deal of the original material in an audio presentation on my blog site (http://www.dickb-blog.com/audio). Anne shared its contents many many mornings at the Smith home with A.A. pioneers and their families.

Its contents were the subject of discussion at the regular Wednesday meetings. Those contents deal with the Biblical, Oxford Group, and Shoemaker roots of A.A. They deal with every single point Bill Wilson dealt with in his Big Book. They include Anne's recommendations and observations for early A.A. members and families about the Bible, about the Christian literature they should read, and about dealing effectively with newcomers. For my own writings and views, see Dick B. *Anne Smith's Journal, 1933-1939*, 3rd ed (Kihei, HI: Paradise Research Publications, Inc., 1998), and *The Akron Genesis of Alcoholics Anonymous*, 2d ed. (Kihei, HI: Paradise Research Publications, Inc., 1998)—summarized in http://www.dickb.com/titles.shtml

.

Typical of the scanty and inadequate treatment of Anne Smith and her A.A. role by the recovery community is the chapter about her in Hazelden's recent *Women Pioneers In 12 Step Recovery*, at pages 1 to 23. That piece cites no sources for its statements. It cans materials from works already written about Anne, Bob, Bill, and others. And it fails completely to report the materials in Anne Smith's Journal. But there is no excuse whatever for such an omission. The anonymous author and his publishers could easily have obtained complete copies of the journal from me, from their own Director of Historical Information, from the archivist at Dr. Bob's Home (at the time of that writing), from the archives at A.A. General Services in New York (where I obtained mine with the help and recommendation of Dr. Bob's daughter Sue Smith Windows), and from either of Dr. Bob's children–Sue Smith Windows in Akron and Robert R. Smith in Texas. Yet where is that history! Why is it consistently ignored! Why have writers and purported historians failed to publish or report or review that document in view of its ready accessibility since I dredged it up in 1991!

I do not know the answer. I do know that A.A. and its purported historians have utterly failed Anne Ripley Smith–the woman Bill Wilson and others called "Mother of A.A."

No one (who purports to write the history of A.A. or to discuss its spiritual program, or to publish biographies of its founders, or to analyze why early A.A. worked) should ever have failed, or fail today, to discuss the writings, teachings, quiet times, practices, and contributions of Anne. One of the best histories I have read is by Pulitzer Prize Winner Nan Robertson. *Getting Better Inside Alcoholics Anonymous* (NY: Fawcett Crest, 1988). I know that she spent substantial time with the pioneers who counted. Her third chapter is titled "The Early Christians"–a truthful description (by a Jewish author, at that) that would scarcely attract much interest in today's A.A. frame of mind. She tells of the Christian books that were read. She points to the extent the early drunks relied on the Bible, particularly the Sermon on the Mount, 1 Corinthians 13, and the Book of James. She points to the detour emanating from Professor William James's writings–a man about whom she declared: "The philosopher's view of God was not Christian." She pointed to Bill's use of the professor's ideas. But Nan correctly and well describes: (1) the unique Akron surrenders where the prospect gave over his life "to the care and direction of the Creator," (2) the prospect's prayer on his knees, and (3) the prospect's new status as a "member" once the surrender was complete. She confirmed what I have reported about quiet times, the sessions with Anne at the Smith home, and readings from the Bible. Robertson said that Dr. Bob's son said of meetings, "It was kind of like an old-fashioned revival meeting" (p. 50). Alas, however, this fine writer did not appear to know about or report on Anne Smith's Journal.

More obvious omissions can be found in the following varied historical accounts: (1) William L. White. *Slaying The Dragon: The History of Addiction Treatment and Recovery in America.* (Illinois: Chestnut Health Systems, 1998). Though processing and reproducing the standard distorted history of A.A., the author scarcely says a word about Anne or her journal. (2) The noted A.A. historian Ernest Kurtz wrote *Not-God: A History of Alcoholics Anonymous*. Exp ed. (MN: Hazelden, 1991). His bow to Anne and her journal is confined to footnote 32 on page 331, where he correctly states that Wilson's alleged "six steps" were not derived from the Oxford Group and cites an "extensively annotated copy of Anne Smith's OG "workbook" in A.A. archives." Period! (3) Then there is Bill's own *Alcoholics Anonymous Comes of Age*. This piece became, for years, the only significant A.A. history. That book contains no mention of Anne's Journal (which was *not* an Oxford Group workbook as some, including Kurtz, have described it); nor does Wilson's history give any significant attention to Anne herself. Similar vacuity exists in almost every other account–whether by Christian, atheist, or academic writers.

**Henrietta Buckler Seiberling and Her Spiritual Infusion**

Bill Wilson said he received a much needed spiritual infusion from Anne Smith and from Henrietta Seiberling while he was in Akron.

Today's A.A. members may possibly have heard the name Seiberling. Perhaps in connection with rubber tires. Perhaps in connection with Congressman John Seiberling, a Democrat, who long served the Akron constituency for the area in which he was reared. But they'd be hard-pressed to answer a quiz about the nature and person of the lady who sparked the membership of Dr. Bob and Anne Smith in the Oxford Group and later A.A. itself.

The lady was Henrietta Buckler Seiberling, the wife of–though separated from–one of the children of Akron's founding rubber tire industry family. To make a long story short, this lady gathered together the Oxford Group friends of Dr. Bob. All–including Bob–prayed for his recovery from alcoholism. Henrietta was quick to recognize what God had wrought in answer to the prayers when she soon received a telephone appeal from the about-to-stray Bill Wilson in Akron. Henrietta quickly introduced Bill to Dr. Bob in her own home on the grounds of the Seiberling Estate.

Henrietta participated a great deal in the development of early A.A. and in helping alcoholics to learn about the Bible, Christianity, and God. She "called the shots" at many of the early Akron meetings. She was mentioned briefly by Wilson as being one of the three-some (Dr. Bob, Anne, and Henrietta) who were having great success helping alcoholics and developing the A.A. program in the Akron crucible. Henrietta Seiberling attended and often led early meetings, studied the Bible and read from it, taught from Christian literature and devotionals, and conferred personally with the early drunks–including Bill Wilson. She certainly helped shape the program and success of early A.A.

My work on Henrietta Seiberling can be found in Dick B. *The Akron Genesis of Alcoholics Anonymous*. I also wrote Henrietta's biography contained in Hazelden's *Women Pioneers In 12 Step Recovery*, *supra*, pp. 25-41. Very recently, on the occasion of the opening of the Seiberling Gate Lodge in Akron (where Henrietta introduced Bill W. and Dr. Bob), I wrote a much more extensive title about Henrietta and her important Akron role. See Dick B. *Henrietta B. Seiberling: Ohio's Lady with a Cause*. 3rd ed. Kihei, HI: Paradise Research Publications, Inc., 2006.

**Eleanor Napier Forde (Newton)–The Inspirations from an Oxford Group Woman Activist**

As you wind your way through the hundreds of Oxford Group books, as I have, you'll often see mention of Eleanor Napier Forde. I came to know her well as a friend during my research and was asked to call her "Ellie." Ellie was from Canada. She lived beyond 100 years of age–topping even Bob Hope and George Burns. A sturdy, active, and devoted Christian she was!

Ellie was the first woman to travel internationally with the Groups and was for many many years a confidant and supporter of Frank Buchman. With 29 others, she joined Buchman on an extended tour of South Africa–informing people about the Four Absolutes, about "listening to God," about their need to get down on their knees and give their lives to God, and about the necessity for their going forth to change other people.

Ellie first heard Reverend Sam Shoemaker preach way back in the early 1920's–before Sam came to Calvary Church in 1925. She soon sought him out and worked for him. Sam then sent her to assist Dr. Frank Buchman. In the Oxford Group, she led a team to Canada. She went to South Africa. She was among the few women who was actually a leader and confidant in the Groups. Ultimately, she met and married Oxford Group activist James Draper Newton, who brought the Oxford Group's influence to A.A. in Akron. She wrote one of the earliest important pieces of Oxford Group literature, *The Guidance of God*. Her first presentation of its ideas was in a pamphlet she wrote in 1927. She spoke at hundreds of Oxford Group meetings, house parties, and team meetings. Her ideas were so much respected that they are quoted at some length by Dr. Bob's wife in *Anne Smith's Journal*.

I list Eleanor Forde Newton as a woman pioneer for several reasons. Most assuredly, she was not an alcoholic. She was never connected with or to A.A. Nor was she an Akron resident. But she gave stature to the leadership by women in early Akron A.A. Her comments (though without attribution) can be found in early A.A. writings. Celebrating her 100$^{th}$ birthday with her venerable husband Jim Newton, she was still living the Christian life, supporting the Oxford Group work and principles, and helping to bring to the fore the real Oxford Group principles from Sam Shoemaker and Frank Buchman that impacted so heavily on both New York and Akron A.A.

For my work discussing Eleanor Forde, see *The Akron Genesis of Alcoholics Anonymous*, 2d ed., *supra*; *The Oxford Group and Alcoholics Anonymous*, 2d ed., *supra*; and *New Light on Alcoholism*, *supra*. For other works highlighting the importance of Eleanor Forde Newton in the Oxford Group, see Garth Lean. *Frank Buchman: a Life* (London:

Constable, 1985), pp. 132, 140-41, 159, 166, 194, 307, 471; Morris H. Martin. *Always A Little Further: Four Lives of a Luckie Felowe* (AZ: Elm Street Press, 2001); Eleanor Forde. *I Always Wanted Adventure* (London: Grosvenor, 1992); *Echoes from the Heart* (Fort Myers Beach, Florida, 1986); *Guidance: What It Is and How to Get It* (Paper presented by Eleanor Napier Forde at Minnewaska, NY, September, 1927); *The Guidance of God* (London: The Oxford Group, 1927); and James D. Newton. *Uncommon Friends* (NY: Harcourt Brace, 1987).

# 4

# The Real Spiritual Roots of Early A.A.'s Program of Recovery

## The Seven Major Biblical Roots

Dr. Bob said quite plainly that A.A.'s basic ideas came from the Bible. Bill Wilson said his Twelve Steps came primarily from Oxford Group principles as taught by Reverend Sam Shoemaker, Rector of Calvary Episcopal Church in New York. In turn, the Oxford Group had long said with equal clarity and conviction that its principles were the principles of the Bible. Shoemaker himself was often called a "Bible Christian." Both Bill Wilson and Dr. Bob frequently declared that Jesus's sermon on the mount (Matthew 5, 6, 7) contained the underlying A.A. philosophy. Hence it is virtually impossible to begin a discussion of A.A.'s "spiritual" roots without stating flatly that they are Biblical in origin, form, and content. Regrettably, most today neither concede these facts or even know them. Some quarantine them as "Protestant."

**The Bible** (See Dick B., *The Good Book and The Big Book; http://www.dick.com/goodbook.shtml)*

Over and over, the historical facts about A.A. establish that the Bible itself was the source of A.A.'s basic ideas. The most important focus in Akron A.A. was Jesus's Sermon on the Mount (Matthew 5, 6, and 7), 1 Corinthians 13, and the Book of James. Extensive guidance and commentary on what was studied in these segments can be found in my title *Why Early A.A. Succeeded* (Kihei, HI: Paradise Research Publications, Inc., 2001) and my recent title *The James Club and The Original A.A. Program's Absolute Essentials*. Most assuredly, other parts of the Bible were stressed as well. There was the life of Christ–particularly as set forth in the four Gospels. There was the Book of Acts–which Anne Smith highly recommended. There certainly was study of the Ten Commandments and Jesus' Two Great Commandments on love of God and of neighbor (even "thine enemy"). And attention was given to the need for a new birth (John 3); receiving the gift of the Holy

Spirit (Acts and Corinthians); healing, forgiveness, and redemption (Psalm 103); repentance (Acts); guidance (James); salvation (Romans); belief in God (Hebrews 11:6); and so on.

**Quiet Time** (See Dick B., *Good Morning!: Quiet Time, Morning Watch, Meditation, and Early A.A.; http://www.dickb.com/goodmorn.shtml*)

First, the observer of quiet time practices, was to become a Christian. The born-again A.A. newcomer was to grow in knowledge, principles, and practices by starting with the Bible. He was to study it. He was to cultivate the habit of prayer. He was to seek the guidance of Yahweh, the Creator. He was advised to read Christian books and use daily devotionals. Books on the life of Christ were especially recommended. Quiet Time–which included all of these for the believer–involved individual work, work with Anne Smith at Dr. Bob's Home, and group quiet times at the regular meetings.

**Anne Smith's Journal** (See Dick B., *Anne Smith's Journal, 1933-1939; http://www.dickb.com/annesm.shtml*)

You will hear me say and you will see me write many times about Anne Smith as the most forgotten and ignored source of A.A.'s Biblical ideas. Hopefully this situation will not continue much longer.

Anne says it all. She shared it all. She was the real "recorder" as far as memorializing in detail the ideas used in Akron and which simply must have impacted on Bill Wilson. She wrote them down in organized fashion in 64 pages from 1933 to 1939. And she shared abundantly from her journal with A.A. members and their families. No purported 12 Step historian today should ever fail to specify Anne Ripley Smith's role, describe Anne Smith's Journal, relate what Anne did with early pioneers and their families, and point to specifics in the pages of Anne's notes.

**The Teachings of Rev. Sam Shoemaker** (See Dick B., *New Light on Alcoholism; http://www.dickb.com/newlight.shtml*)

Take note that Bill Wilson ultimately attributed practically all the Twelve Steps and their ideas to Reverend Shoemaker. Sam was a Bible Christian. Bill called Sam a co-founder of A.A. Bill even asked Sam to write the Twelve Steps, but Sam declined. Sam was asked to, and did, review Bill's first Big Book manuscripts before they were published. And Sam's words, language, and ideas can be found in the Steps and throughout the

Big Book. See also Dick B., *Twelve Steps for You* (Kihei, HI: Paradise Research Publications, Inc., 2005); *By the Power of God, supra*; and Bill P. and Dick B., *Courage to Change* (Hazelden); and Appendix 2 in this title.

**The Life-Changing Program of the Oxford Group** (See Dick B., *The Oxford Group and Alcoholics Anonymous; http://www.dickb.com/Oxford.shtml*

Try though he did, Bill Wilson could not and cannot distance his writings or his Big Book from the Oxford Group. As we wrote, the principles of the Oxford Group were the principles of the Bible. The simple fact is that Wilson's whole "program" is Oxford Group in character, principles, practices, and language.

Wilson changed Oxford Group words that he used, but not the ideas they expressed. Wilson deleted well-known expressions such as The Five C's, The Four Absolutes, Restitution, and so on. Wilson eliminated Jesus Christ from the process. But Bill worked closely with Sam Shoemaker in the formative years. By contrast, Dr. Bob scarcely was in contact with Sam. Yet Bob and his wife, Henrietta Seiberling, and Mr. And Mrs. T. Henry Williams were avid readers of Oxford Group literature and were thoroughly conversant with its ideas. See also Dick B., *By the Power of God, supra; Twelve Steps for You, supra;* and *Utilizing Early A.A.'s Spiritual Roots for Recovery Today (http://www.dickb.com/titles.shtml)*

**The Christian Literature Early A.A. Members Read** (See Dick B., *The Books Early A.A.'s Read for Spiritual Growth; http://www.dickb.com/titlees)*

The Akron pioneers were readers of Biblical literature. Dr. Bob was a reader. And, contrary to common belief–including my own until recently–Bill Wilson was a reader. Akron people were spurred on in their reading by Dr. Bob, Anne, and Henrietta. They read the Bible. They read Christian devotionals– *The Runner's Bible, The Upper Room, My Utmost for His Highest.* They read "inspirational" books like *As A Man Thinketh, The Greatest Thing in the World,* Fox's *The Sermon on the Mount,* Kagawa's *Love: The Law of Life*, Charles Sheldon's *In His Steps*, and titles by many great religious leaders–Glenn Clark, E. Stanley Jones, Oswald Chambers, Harry Emerson Fosdick, Norman Vincent Peale, Henry Drummond, and countless others. They read Sam Shoemaker's titles and pamphlets. They read the Oxford Group books (of which by the year 2003, I had uncovered more than 500 in all). And you can find references to these pieces of Biblical literature in A.A.'s *Cleveland Central Bulletin*, the *AA Grapevine*, and the Akron AA pamphlets we've mentioned. See also Dick B., *Dr. Bob and His Library;* and *Making Known the Biblical Roots of A.A.*

**United Christian Endeavor Society principles and practices.** See Dick B., *The James Club and The Original A.A. Program's Absolute Essentials;* http://www.dickb.com/JamesClub.shtml.

Only recently did I add this seventh major root because only recently did I begin extensive research on what Dr. Bob meant when he said he had received "excellent training" in the Bible as a youngster and recited the number of times he went to church each week as a youngster. As previously stated, the Christian Endeavor ideas of confession of Christ, Bible study meetings, prayer meetings, conversion meetings, Quiet Hour, topical discussions of religious literature, love and service have convinced me of their major impact on the actual Akron program of the pioneer Christian Fellowship.

## Other "Spiritual" Roots

**Carl Jung**. Though a psychiatrist, Dr. Jung's ideas on "conversion" were foundational in A.A.

**William James**. Though a philosopher and psychologist, William James presented some ideas that impacted heavily on Bill Wilson, and even Sam Shoemaker. James was not a Christian. He had his own ideas about a god and religion. He was a major contributor to the "higher power" stuff in A.A. His definition of "self-surrender," and of the "turning point," were directly incorporated into A.A. thinking by Wilson. Though James was long dead at the time of A.A.'s founding, Bill Wilson called James a founder and claimed that James was the author of Bill's First Step concept of "deflation at depth." None of these ideas could be called Christian or Biblical in nature or content

**Richard Peabody and *The Common Sense of Drinking*.**

Many have tried to associate the "Emanuel Movement" with the spiritual roots of A.A. But any careful study should have shown them that the Emanuel techniques had far more to do with psychology than with religion, even though one of their authors wrote much on spiritual healing. The problem is, that A.A. appears to have taken nothing from these people. On the other hand, Richard Peabody, the lay therapist, could be called an offshoot of the Emanuel group. Peabody's lay ideas about relaxation, the lack of a cure, the need for a "surrender" and some of the expressions in his *The Common Sense of Drinking* were appropriated by Wilson in the language of the Big Book as Bill saw it. But the Peabody link was anything but "spiritual" or "successful." For Peabody did not rely on God in his treatment, and he died drunk–thus confirming that there was no cure—for him at least!

In a very real sense, the irrelevance of the "spiritual" side of any Emanuel link parallels the irrelevance of the "spiritual" side of the Washingtonian Movement of the previous century. Much has been made of these two historical phenomena; but neither offered anything significant as to God's power to heal, nor any success record that indicated the techniques were effective in a way that meant anything to Bill and Bob. The early movement was a temperance pledge outfit which placed no reliance on the Creator–and vanished. The other movement talked about God a little, but it spawned work that was primarily in the psychological treatment realm; and in the case of Peabody, was a big flop!

**The "New Thought" Crowd**. There are traces in the reading and thinking of early A.A. members taken from New Though writers like Ralph Waldo Emerson, Phineas P.Quimby, Mary Baker Eddy, Ralph Waldo Trine, James Allen, Emmet Fox, Charles Fillmore, Horatio W. Dresser, F. L. Rawson, Thomas Troward, and others.

**The "Farther Out" Crowd**. Still other writers, who could be called "farther out" or on the periphery of conventional religion, touched the A.A. scene. There were people like Emmanuel Swedenborg. There were psychic healers. There were spiritualist writers. And you can find their tracks in some of Bill's bizarre words and phrases like "higher power," "Spirit of the Universe," "Creative Intelligence," "Universal Mind," "Spirit of Nature," "Czar of the Heavens," "Power," "Presence of Infinite Power and Love," "sunlight of the Spirit," "the world of the Spirit," and "fourth dimension of existence." You can find some of their books among Dr. Bob's pile of reading, and you can find some in the "spook room" at Bill and Lois's Stepping Stones home.

Consider that Dr. Bob said A.A.'s basic ideas came from study of the Bible. Also that Rev. Sam Shoemaker was Bill's spiritual teacher in the developmental days. He was, as well, a solid Bible teacher. Remember too that Bill Wilson often extracted words and phrases from Shoemaker's teachings and even from the Bible itself–though never giving the source. Consider these facts if you like. But some of Bill's words make you feel more like you are studying theosophy or walking in his "spook room" than "borrowing religious ideas that are the common property of mankind," as Bill liked to claim.

## Bill Wilson's Tight Rope

Perhaps the devil is farther into the A.A. mix than most understand. Bill was walking on a tight rope when he undertook an explanation of Christian healings. He wrote from, and was hampered by, some unusual background factors.

Bill had been an atheist. He had probably accepted Christ while drunk at the Rescue Mission. At the very best, he walked as a carnal Christian in most areas of his life–spiritualism, psychic studies, depression, LSD, adultery, money shenanigans, and other "sins" which often accompany alcoholism. Moreover, this behavior continued long into Bill's "sobriety." Bill wanted to sell books for royalties to any and every drunk–whatever that drunk's belief system or religion might turn out to be. Later, he took the same view about selling his Vitamin B 3 Therapy.

On the other side of the picture, Bill wrote as one who had great respect for his co-founding partner–the Christian Bible student, Dr. Bob. Moreover he had been commissioned to write a text about how the Christian Akron program reported out by Frank Amos had actually worked. Further, perhaps, to the confusion of the untrained and unchurched Bill, most of his non-Biblical sources quoted, paraphrased, and even distorted Scripture at some length. So did the devil, but Jesus countered with "It is written" and answered bad Scripture with appropriate Scripture–something Wilson was not prepared on his own to do. And the non-Biblical writers he quoted or mentioned were certainly presenting unconventional ideas if their ideas are compared to those of theologians and writers about Biblical Christianity. See Dick B., *Cured: Proven Help for Alcoholics and Addicts*; *God and Alcoholism: Our Challenge in the 21st Century*, pp. 77-118; and *Making Known the Biblical Roots of A.A.* (http://www.dickb.com/makingknown.shtml)/

## Confusions among the Conclusions

Several Christian writers have tackled the confusing non-Christian "theology" apparent in Bill Wilson's writings. Our bibliography provides the names and titles of these people. Unfortunately, most of these writers incorporate some serious misconceptions about A.A., the Bible, the Oxford Group, Dr. Bob, and Bill. Nonetheless, they correctly perceive some vital deficiencies in any contention that A.A. is Christian or even was Christian.

Two of the most critical writers are Martin and Deidre Bobgan. See *12 Steps To Destruction* (Santa Barbara, CA: East Gate Publishers, 1992). Personally, I disagree strongly with some of the Bobgan conclusions, and I certainly believe they spend too much time criticizing the Oxford Group instead of examining and correctly reporting the Akron program from reliable sources such as the Frank Amos reports. They just plain miss the historical facts when it comes to the Biblical focus in Akron, the teachings of Rev. Sam Shoemaker, and the Christian literature that predominated in the Akron program.

Nonetheless, the following statements in the Bobgans' book are very helpful in understanding A.A. confusion that does exist:

> Bill Wilson's moralizing throughout his essays on the Twelve Steps may further confuse people. Some of his talk about prayer even sounds Christian. He picked up the language of prayer with the Thee's and Thou's during his early contact with the Oxford Group, and he made prayer a daily practice. Nevertheless, it is abundantly clear that "God as we understood Him" is not the Triune God of the Bible, who has revealed Himself and who has declared that He is the Only God and there are no others. Thus when Wilson talks about praying to God, it is not at all clear that he is referring to Almighty God. Likewise, when he talks about prayer and meditation and conscious contact with God, he does not limit himself exclusively to Christian prayer, Christian meditation, and relationship to Jesus Christ. Many people pray to other gods and practice meditation. Many believe they are contacting God when in fact they are contacting other spirits [*12 Steps to Destruction, supra*, pp. 217-18].

> Wilson placed great confidence in matters of spirituality that are forbidden by Scripture. As mentioned earlier, he was involved in necromancy (contacting the dead), using the Ouija board, and channeling messages. . . . Wilson wrote the following: "Throughout A.A., we find a large amount of psychic phenomena, nearly all of it

> spontaneous. Alcoholic after alcoholic tells me of such experiences and asks if these denote lunacy–or do they have real meaning? These psychic experiences have run nearly the full gamut of everything we see in the books. In addition to my original mystic experience, I've had a lot of such phenomenalism myself [*12 Steps to Destruction*, *supra*, p. 218].

I'll tell you frankly that I have no interest in the mixed up nonsense and serious spiritual sickness evidenced by Wilson's remarks. Nor would I want to analyze them or prosecute them. When I visited his home at Stepping Stones, I was introduced to the "spook room" on the right side of the front room as you entered the cottage. Its "library" was filled with psychic baloney, but it is a credit to Stepping Stones that they left it there for people to see and judge for themselves. However, I was asked not to investigate Wilson's locked files and records that pertained to Bill's spiritualism and drug use; and I honored that request. In those days, I had no interest in such stuff. And I still don't. But knowledge of it has become more important as you watch A.A.'s drift from the Bible to New Age mysticism—impelled to some extent by Wilson's popularity and open embracing of such stuff. The fact of its existence is clearly recorded in and out of A.A. literature. See Robertson, *Getting Better Inside Alcoholics Anonymous*, *supra*, pp. 32, 124; *Pass It On* NY: Alcoholics Anonymous World Services, 1984, pp. 275-80, 301, 368-77.

Unlike Wilson, I have not had alcoholic after alcoholic tell me about mystic experiences or about any of Wilson's other spiritually sick stuff. As a matter of fact, I have had alcoholic after alcoholic write me looking for the accurate facts about A.A.'s Christian roots. Some have said their ministers were much affronted by Wilson's drug use, seances, and psychic experimentation; but the main interest of the inquiring A.A. people themselves was in the Bible and how to use it in A.A. That, I believe, is a totally worthwhile mission today. The tragedy is that, when you mix the not-god revisionism in current A.A. with Wilsonian spiritualism and hookey pook, you multiply the confusing ideas that appear to be heavily contributing to A.A.'s plummeting success rates.

That does bother me! We are ignoring God, the Bible, and Jesus Christ and exalting idolatry, New Age nonsense, and spiritual confusion. And with no logic, success record, or Biblical accuracy to justify it. None!

# 5

# Who Let the Goofy Gods into A.A.?

When the President of the United States says: "God Bless America," he is not referring to a "Something" or a "Somebody" or an "it." He *is* speaking about the Creator. When the kids say a Pledge of Allegiance to the American Flag and say "one nation under God," they are not referring to "Ralph" or Santa Claus or a chair or a light bulb. They are speaking about the Creator. When the Declaration of Independence said that "that they are endowed by their Creator with certain unalienable Rights," it did not mean that they were endowed by a radiator or Gertrude or the Big Dipper.

When, how, and by whom, therefore, did A.A. go goofy, and go for goofy gods? Its Big Book does not refer to "Somebody." Its Twelve Steps do not refer to Gertrude or Ralph. The Serenity Prayer which opens most meetings makes no mention of Santa Claus. And the Lord's Prayer which closes most meetings is not addressing "Our Radiator." Who, pray tell, let the goofy gods into A.A.! Dr. Bob never spoke of a Big Dipper or an A.A. group in the same breath as Heavenly Father.

## First, Who Is God As Early AAs Spoke of Him?

Bill Wilson answered this question over 400 times in his basic text *Alcoholics Anonymous.* Even in the Fourth Edition of the Big Book–just published–Bill said, "And it means, of course, that we are going to talk about God." *Alcoholics Anonymous*, 4$^{th}$ ed., page 45.

Who is this very "God" about whom Bill Wilson spoke so many times? The undeniable answer is that the "God" of early A.A. was unquestionably "God" as named, defined, and described in the Good Book. And both Bill Wilson and Bob Smith used very precise Biblical terms that make that clear.

The word "God" with a capital "G" is used over 200 times in the Big Book, 3$^{rd}$ edition, as counted and documented by several Big Book analysts and as can be established by a reading of Poe's *Concordance to Alcoholics Anonymous.*

Descriptions of God, as they are used in the Bible, appear over and over in A.A.'s basic text and other literature. These include: Creator, Maker, Almighty, Spirit, Father, Father of lights, God of our fathers, and Heavenly Father.

Note that "God" is a title, but not a personal name. The Creator's personal name is Yahweh. See Appendix 1 of this title. Perhaps neither Dr. Bob nor Bill Wilson could have been expected to see the trap door that was opened when Wilson inserted other appellations which may have been music to the ears of unbelievers and humanists but has confused A.A. members for decades. Had Dr. Bob and Bill used God's personal name Yahweh, there could have been no room for the idolatrous other "gods" that have crept into today's A.A. And why?

The Creator explicitly declared His personal name in the Bible, and that name appears in the texts over 7,000 times–though not properly translated in most versions. The Creator's personal name is *Yahweh.* It is not "God." It is not "Jehovah." It is not "Adonai." It is not "Lord." It is Yahweh. See Dick B., *Why Early A.A. Succeeded: The Good Book in Alcoholics Anonymous Yesterday and Today* (Kihei, HI: Paradise Research Publications, 2001), pp. 55-72, 209-23; Appendix 1 of this title; for, as the *New Jerusalem Bible* states in Exodus 3:15:

> And God also said to Moses, "You are to say to the sons of Israel: Yahweh, the God of your fathers, the God of Abraham, the God of Isaac, and the God of Jacob has sent me to you. This is my name for all time; by this name shall I be invoked for all generations to come."

The Creator provided and commanded the use of His personal name for all generations to come. Yahweh also commanded in Exodus 20:3-5:

> Thou shalt have no other gods before me.
> Thou shalt not make unto thee any graven image, or any likeness *of any thing* that *is* in heaven above, or that *is* in the earth beneath, or that *is* in the water under the earth.
> Thou shalt not bow down thyself to them, nor serve them: for I the LORD [Yahweh] thy God *am* a jealous God, visiting the iniquity of the fathers upon the children unto the third and fourth *generation* of them that hate me.

Psalm 115 tells Israel who Yahweh is, where He is, and what He has done. It contrasts the gods of the heathen, pointing out that they are mere silver and gold–the work of men's hands, speak not, see not, hear not, smell not, handle not, and walk not. In fact, they fully qualify as the goofy gods of A.A. centuries later–door knobs, light bulbs, chairs, radiators, etc. Underlining the importance He assigned to His personal name, Yahweh commanded:

> Thou shalt not take the name of the LORD [Yahweh in the texts] thy God in vain; for the Lord will not hold him guiltless that has taken his name in vain (Exod. 20:7).
>
> And ye shall not swear by my name falsely, neither shalt thou profane the name of thy God. I am the LORD [Yahweh in the texts] (Lev. 19:12).
>
> Glory ye in his holy name: let the heart of them rejoice that seek the LORD [Yahweh in the texts] (Ps. 105:3).
>
> So will I make my holy name known in the midst of my people Israel; and I will not let them pollute my holy name any more: and the heathen shall know that I am the LORD [Yahweh in the texts], the Holy One of Israel (Ezek. 39:7).

The Creator--Yahweh, our God--never intended that there be doubt as to Who He is, what His personal name is, that He is the only true and living God, and that He abhors false gods and idols–whether they are silver, gold, radiators, light bulbs, or groups.

Lest you think the foregoing is useless, subjective Bible thumping, let's consider the following *descriptions* of Yahweh, the Creator, in the Good Book. These descriptions are not only in the Bible, but in the Big Book, and frequently in the words of Bill Wilson and Dr. Bob:

> *The living God* (Jer. 10:10; Matt. 16:16, Acts 14:15, Rom. 9:26, 2 Cor. 3:3; 6:16, 1 Tim. 4:10).
>
> *Almighty God* (Gen. 17:1. 35:11; Exod. 6:3; Ezek. 10:5; Rev. 15:3).
>
> *God our Father* (Rom. 1:7; 1 Cor. 1:3; 2 Cor. 1:2; Eph. 1:2; Phil. 1:2; 2 Thess. 1:1)

*Heavenly Father* (Matt. 6:32)
*Father of Light* (from James 1:17)

*Creator* (Eccl. 12:1)

*Maker* (Psalm 95:6)

*Father* (Matt. 5:45)

*Spirit* (John 4:24)

The founders used other Biblical terms referring to Yahweh–terms such as "God of our fathers," "Love," "Light," God of Grace, and Father of Mercies.

For the life of me, I cannot imagine scholars, writers, professors, and historians converting the foregoing Bible terms into a light bulb, a goddess, a door knob, an Ouija board, a tarot card, a gargoyle, or a totem pole. There may be those today who go for that stuff. But they did not belong to the A.A. Christian Fellowship in Akron, Ohio. You'd have to be uneducated, prejudiced, skeptical, or just plain blind to think the pioneers did not understand the difference between a totem pole and Yahweh, our Almighty God, the Creator. And if the prospect of looming government intrusion, diminishing insurance money, loss of more patients, or the reduction of book sales is the catalyst for such revisionism and secularization, pity the seemingly hopeless real alcoholic who just wants to get well, but has a light bulb or a tarot card shoved down his throat as a "power" source.

## Second, Bill Injected Substitutionary Words into the Big Book--Which Still Were Not Intended to Mean and Did Not Mean Idols or False gods

Devilish ideas crept into the God scene in early A.A. But they sneaked or were sneaked in the back door. To be sure, Lois Wilson was crying for a "universal" A.A.; but she was neither A.A. nor Christian. To be sure, a rare few in New York cried that there was "too much God" in Bill's proposed Big Book. But some of these were not A.A. or Christian or even sober for long. Nonetheless, at Bill's own urging, A.A. people have been led to believe that some great compromise was fashioned for atheists like Bill. Actually, both the Oxford Group and Rev. Sam Shoemaker liked "standing near the door" which they believed led to God and helped atheists find their way to God via Jesus Christ and a conversion experience. See Helen Smith Shoemaker, *I Stand By The Door: The Life of Sam Shoemaker* (NY: Harper & Row, 1967), pp. ix-x. But there is no evidence that Frank Buchman or Sam Shoemaker or the Oxford Group people of the 1930's were touting the devil or his minions for the leadership of the world. They did talk a lot–too much in fact–about a "God controlled world." But there is not the slightest indication they were seeking to put Lucifer on the throne. I don't think even Bill Wilson thought that.

The trap door that Bill Wilson stuck in his Big Book seemed harmless enough to him, to Ruth Hock (the secretary), to Hank Parkhurst ( Bill's partner), and perhaps to one or two others. Not, however, to the Christian John Henry Fitzhugh Mayo, who was present at compromise time and did not like or support what he saw. What were fashioned were the following seemingly reasonable Oxford Group references to Yahweh that were designed to ease the unbeliever into a new birth. Interestingly, however, at that time there was in circulation the old A.A. saying: "You can ooze your way out of booze, but you can't ooze your way into God." Here, however, were the attempts to do just that:

**God As We Understood Him**

Here's a phrase that Ebby passed along to Bill from the Oxford Group and that Bill used when he made his surrender to God at Towns Hospital just prior to his "hot flash." There was nothing new about the expression. Sam Shoemaker had used it for years and continued to use it in connection with his apologia "So I Stay Near the Door." I discuss its Shoemaker and Oxford Group source at some length in Dick B., *Turning Point: A History of Early A.A.'s Spiritual Roots and Successes*, pp. 171-181.

There are, however, so many uniformed writers and historians who don't know or acknowledge the origin of this phrase that I'll specify just a few of the places in Sam Shoemaker's writings where you can find it - items written long before Bill Wilson got sober:

- S.M. Shoemaker, Jr., *Children of the Second Birth.* NY: Fleming H. Revell Company, 1927: "So they prayed together, opening their minds ***to as much of God as he understood***, removing first the hindrance of self-will. . ." (p. 47). "So he said that he would 'surrender as much of himself as he could, ***to as much of Christ as***

***he understood*'." (p. 25). And note, that Sam was, throughout the book, speaking of a new birth (John 3)–saying of a newcomer's remark: "I do feel reborn, born of the Spirit" (p. 25). At page 32, Shoemaker quoted the Nicodemus story in John 3:1-8, adding the "great truth which he had heard from the Lord, 'Ye *must* be born again'."

- *Sam Shoemaker at his best.* NY: Faith at Work, Inc., 1964: "[R]eal decision and surrender to Christ [is]. . . surrendering 'as much of himself as he can, ***to as much of Christ as he understands'***." (p. 62); "Real faith begins when we surrender ourselves to that God who manifested Himself in Christ, ***giving as much of ourselves as we can to as much of Him as we know.***" (P. 26)

- Samuel M. Shoemaker. *How You Can Help Other People.* Atlanta, GA: Lay Renewal Publications, 1946; "I do not think that anyone ever ***surrendered himself to all he believed about God, without finding God in the process***." (p. 63)

- Samuel Shoemaker. *How To Become a Christian.* NY: Harper & Row Publishers, 1953: "It is so with the decision about Christ. We surrender as much of ourselves as we can ***to as much of Christ as we understand.***" (p. 71)

- Samuel M. Shoemaker. *The Gospel According To You.* NY: Fleming H. Revell Company, 1934: "Surrender to whatever you know about Him, or believe must be the truth about Him. Surrender to Him, if necessary, in total ignorance of Him. ***Far more important that you touch Him than that you understand Him at first***." (p. 128)

Sam Shoemaker intended no trap door into the devil's workplace. His apologia was "So I Stay Near The Door." The key to the surrender Bill Wilson embodied in the revised Third Step was taken directly from Sam Shoemaker's teachings. And you can find many many more expressions in Shoemaker's writings that indicate Shoemaker's belief in the experiment with John 7:17, by which you **"find God" and do so at the beginning by surrendering as much of yourself as you understand to as much of God as you understand.**

No new God. No idol. No idle worship. No door knob. Just a surrender like the one Wilson himself made when he surrendered to God at Towns Hospital. You surrender as much of yourself as you know and understand to as much of God as you know and understand. And then, of course, your try to grow in your understanding of God. There is no rainbow, or radiator or higher power or chair in the picture at all. To say so, would be absurd. Thus Wilson wrote explicitly about his own surrender to God–not to some idol. His words echoed those of Shoemaker as Bill said:

> There I humbly offered myself to God, as I then understood Him, to do with me as He would. I placed myself unreservedly under His care and direction. (*Alcoholics Anonymous*, 1st ed., 1939, p. 22)

Bill surrendered to Almighty God, the Creator, as Bill then understood Him–just as Ebby Thacher had suggested that Bill do. Early A.A. members, including Anne Smith and Oxford Group writers, proposed and used the same technique, suggesting surrender of as much of yourself as you know to as much of God as you know.

**A Power Greater Than Ourselves**

There is with this phrase, but we will not here repeat, the same Shoemaker/Oxford Group source that fostered the phrase God as we understood Him. The "Power" stuff has also been universalized, sanitized, and compromised by revisionists. But Sam Shoemaker and many Oxford Group writers had used this phrase or similar phrases in referring to finding and knowing the Creator. So did Bill Wilson when he spoke of "that power which is God." (*Alcoholics Anonymous*, 4th ed., p. 46). No gargoyles or trees–just this trap door utilized by compromise writers to obscure the fact that the "power greater than ourselves" is Yahweh, our Creator.

**Higher Power**

This monstrosity may have had some good purpose in Bill Wilson's mind. But not for long! And certainly not in the minds of people like Professor William James who used it with abandon and confusing nouns. Originally, as illustrated at pages 43 and 100 of the Fourth Edition of the Big Book, the context referred to Almighty God. A moment's glance at pages 45 and 100 proves that. The reference was to the Creator.

Even the non-Christian Lois Wilson wrote in her diaries about what *God* had done for Bill Wilson. She was not talking about Gertrude or the Big Dipper or a table. And Anne Smith was much more blunt. Not only was

Anne Smith's Journal replete with references to the Bible and the Creator, but she specifically commented that referring to "Christ " as a "group" was a "funk hole"–her observation making clear that talking about a "group" instead of "Christ" is a trap for the unwary and a violation of God's commandments. See Dick B., *Anne Smith's Journal, supra*, pp. 91-92. She said the following was the funk hole: "Using the word 'Group' instead of 'Christ'."

Despite Anne's wise counsel rejecting idolatrous language, the New Thought influences were already in play within Bill's A.A. scene. Ralph Waldo Trine, William James, Emanuel Movement leaders, and Emmet Fox had given the New Thought "higher power" a new status in Bill's mind. The queer higher power phrase was substituted in place of Yahweh our God for some weird god of New Thought manufacture. Some of the writers may still have had Yahweh in mind, but their thinking and reasoning strayed far from biblical Christianity. That has been the New Age approach as well–universalize, secularize, mysticize.

The approach, however, is hardly "new" or merely of this "age." Though I would call it a reversion, it can easily be seen to have a solid root in Freemasonry. Henry C. Clausen, probably the top Masonic leader of the last century, was Sovereign Grand Commander of The Supreme Council, Thirty Third Degree (Mother Supreme Council of the World); Sovereign Grand Inspector General in California; and Past Grand Master of Masons in California. Before his fairly recent death, Clausen revised the monumental morals and dogma work of his predecessor, the renowned Sovereign Grand Commandeer Albert Pike. He published *Clausen's Commentaries on Morals and Dogma*, 2d ed. San Diego, CA: The Supreme Council (Mother Council of the World) of the Inspectors General Knights Commander of the House of the Temple of Solomon of the Thirty-third Decree of the Ancient and Accepted Scottish Rite of Freemasonry of the Southern Jurisdiction of the United States of America, 1976.

Grand Commander Clausen explained the nature, history, and degrees of Scottish Rite. He frequently quotes Professor William James, stating:

> [He gave us a great guide in these words:] "The greatest discovery of my generation is that we have learned we can alter our lives by altering our attitudes of mind" (p. xviii)

Action seems to follow feeling, but really action and feeling go together; and by regulating the action, which is under the more direct control of our will, we can indirectly regulate the feeling, which is not" (p. 170).

[Clausen wrote:] William James, the American giant of psychology, harmonized religion and mysticism, concluding that "personal religious experience has its roots and center in mystical states of consciousness." (p. 210).

The Masonic leader then points to all the factors, upon which the Scottish Rite degrees have drawn: (1) First, the German physicist-philosopher who said,"Mysticism is one of the great discoveries of mankind;" Albert Einstein, who spoke of the profoundness of "the sensation of the mysterious;" Immanuel Kant, the great mystic-philosopher, who said, "there was a higher power, greater than mind power, and that this mysterious force is available for those who will seek beyond the rational;" Thales and Pythagoras, "Initiates in the Greater Mysteries;" Ralph Waldo Emerson; Confucius; Moses; Mohammed; Amenemhat III; and Jesus. (2) Second, the era of Osiris, Krishna, Buddha, Zoraster, Orpheus, Moses, :Pythagoras, and Jesus. (3) Dipping into the Hebrew and Christian books and drawing from the ancient mysteries of Egypt, Persia, Greece, India, the Druids and Essenes, the legends of the Crusades and ceremonies of knighthood. All in all, it is clear from Clausen's treatise that the "Lesser and Greater Mysteries," "The Holy Doctrine–the Royal Secret," and "The Legend of the Egyptian god, Osiris" all were welcome universal, secular, and mystical examples of Masonic symbolism and degrees.

The trends described above, beginning long before the birth of Christ and extending to the higher powers of today, present convincing arguments that A.A. is far more today than a Christian Fellowship, an offshoot of Christian Endeavor, or a Bible-thumping prayer group.

And Wilson capped it off after Dr. Bob's death by telling A.A. members that their A.A. group could be their higher power–exactly what Anne Smith's had said would be a "funk hole." And it most assuredly has been just that! A.A. jargon today speaks of more weird gods than either the ancient Greeks or ancient Romans.

## Enter the "goofy gods" through the Back Door

I don't think any early A.A. ever dreamed of the distortions that would come from "as we understood Him" and "power greater than ourselves" and "higher power." But the distortions have flowed freely from the mouths of today's A.A. members, recovery writers, rehabs, therapists, and professionals. In book after book that I have written, I have pointed to those "scholars," "historians," "therapists," and peripatetic story tellers who have given a new and exalted meaning to the nonsense gods of recovery. No kidding. The names I list below are no invention of mine. They are absurd. Sam Shoemaker himself warned AAs about "absurd names for God." Yet the names below have been used with reference to the Creator upon whom early pioneers relied for recovery and for their cures. And just how silly can they be? Well, here are documented examples of what these nonsense (goofy) gods have been said to be:

> A light bulb. A coke bottle. Santa Claus. The Big Dipper. Good Orderly Direction. Group of Drunks. An A.A. group. A chair. A table. A radiator. A goddess. A door knob. Someone. Something. "Him, Her, or It." A not-god. Your self. A "higher power." Ralph. Gertrude. A rock. That-which-keeps-you-sober, and Nothing at all.

The foregoing are "certified" "higher powers" in today's absurd recovery writing, program, and therapy nomenclature. I've heard and seen them all in A.A. literature, in recovery literature, in medical literature, in religious literature, and in government pamphlets and releases. Some are discussed in more detail in Dick B., *The Golden Text of A.A.: God, the Pioneers, and Real Spirituality*. (Kihei, HI: Paradise Research Publications, 1999). Also in Dick B., *God and Alcoholism,* Kihei, HI: Paradise Research Publications, Inc.

## A. A. People May Be Sick, but They Are Not Stupid

How any well-intentioned person would attempt to saddle very sick alcoholics and addicts with such baloney, I cannot explain. Newly sober alcoholics may be sick, but they are not stupid. Their sickness–and mine in years gone by–made them receptive to almost any idea that was passed on authoritatively, or as "spirituality," or by way of the prejudicial mocking of "religion."

When you are new, it's easier to go along with the gang. If the gang says you can make a door knob your higher power, why argue! If the gang says you can believe whatever you like and even have no faith at all, why argue! If the gang says A.A. is a "spiritual, but not religious program," why argue! The answer and the major point to keep in mind today: You'll get verbally trounced if you dissent. The appeal to stupidity has grown more and more forceful as the distance from early A.A. has grown farther and farther.

It's not too hard to understand Dr. Bob's admonition to Bill: "Keep it simple." Bill was an ex-drunk with limited sobriety, with no experience in a church or with the Bible or even in the Oxford Group. He had been pelted with ideas from Carl Jung, William James, William Silkworth, Richard Peabody, Sam Shoemaker, Frank Buchman, Emmet Fox and other New Thought writers, and perhaps even with the Masonic mysticism which might have crept into Dr. Bob's expressions. Bob was a Thirty-second degree Scottish Rite Mason. He was a Christian, a Bible student, a church-goer, and an active participant in Christian Endeavor. He was highly educated. He was a voracious reader–of Confucius, Unity, Christian Science, Fosdick, Clark, psychic healers, spiritualists, Sam Shoemaker, Oxford Group writings, Roman Catholic writings, New Thought writings, and plenty of New Thought writings. Still Bob kept his devotions simple, his prayer life simple, his teachings simple, his derivations from the Bible simple, and his meetings simple. He seemed to be able to handle the challenge of the various ideas with which he was familiar and with which Bill, perhaps, had become enamored but not much of a student. And a price was paid in letting Bill stuff it all in the language of the Big Book and Steps. Bill didn't keep it simple. Certainly not when he introduced his higher powers, fourth dimensions, etc.

Not long ago, therapies, treatment centers, and recovery books seemed to be at their peak. You could pass off just about anything as "god" while the patients meandered through the halls. You could include any like-minded group in the category of a Twelve Step program–whatever its beliefs. You could draw insurance money if you just kept it all broad enough, A.A. enough, and "spiritual" enough to offend no one. You could receive government assistance. You could establish yourself as a counselor, whatever your background or training. But, I believe, this casual reference to some illusory power is no longer doing the job. Not with impunity. Things are changing–for a variety of reasons.

First of all, the courts are ruling the obvious: A.A. is a religion. God is God. Spirituality is a cop-out for faith. See Stanton Peele and Charles Bufe and Archie Brodsky. *Resisting 12-Step Coercion: How To Fight Participation in AA, NA, or 12-Step Treatment.* (Tucson, AZ: See Sharp Press, 2000), pp. 107-158. I don't agree with everything these dudes say by a long shot, but they have some powerful evidence and reach some obviously correct conclusions. Second, the insurance companies are apparently recognizing the obvious: A diluted A.A. offers very little to those who pay for, or insure, it in treatment settings. Third, Christian groups are not blind to the idolatry problem. Many refer to the commandment: "Thou shalt have no other gods before me." Fourth, so are Jewish believers who are able and willing to look beyond the Lord's Prayer to their God Yahweh–the very subject of the entire Bible. Fifth, non-Christian secular and atheist groups are recognizing what is clear: A.A. is too religious for them, even though actually lacking in understandable religion. They view A.A. as too spiritual, even though it lacks any definition of what that means, other than reliance on the Creator. They see A.A. as too ritualistic, yet lack proof that the ritual, the meetings, and the joyful conventions are enough to save lives without the very God that they by-pass.

I certainly don't have any answers to these quandaries. I know that A.A. has stopped growing. I know its success rate is abysmally low. I can look around me at meeting after meeting and wonder where the old friends went. I know we have to listen in meetings not merely to the sick and shaky mutterings of new people, but also to the pontifications uttered by a wide variety of proponents of mysticism, spiritualism, higher powers, self-made religion, and absurd names for God. I know that splinter groups within and without A.A. are proliferating, and that you can establish that fact by counting the number of self-help, support, anonymous, para-church, and other fellowships on the scene today. I do know that A.A. had phenomenal success when the Creator was the focus of its reliance. Yet even that fact is under fire by AA "history lovers." And I do ponder Bill Wilson's little-known statement to Father John Ford, S.J.–made when Ford had inquired about sanctions against those who were in disagreement with A.A. views (whatever they might be, I guess). And Bill's response was illustrative of his views at that time. He said in substance that he didn't much care what the Buddhists did with the Twelve Steps. And the wisdom in this response, if Bill meant what he wrote, is that A.A. does not have to be, should not be, and will not profit from being, all things to all people. It may extend itself to "all" people; but it has little to offer when it tries to incorporate "all" ideas.

Cure was by conversion for Dr. Carl Jung and Rowland Hazard. It was a decision for Christ for Ebby Thacher. It was manna from heaven for Dr. Bob. It was a "hot flash" experience for Bill. It produced an instantaneous cure for A.A. Number Three once he turned to God for help, and all these provided a creditable record that attracted many a suffering drunk.

## Is There Any Prospect That the Nonsense Will Go

I just scoped out the personal stories in the back of A.A.'s new Fourth Edition of the Big Book. I certainly knew that the higher powers in New York had tossed out many of the old-timer testimonies in earlier editions. I also did not expect to see any mention of the Bible or Jesus Christ. I did expect to see *more* light bulbs, gargoyles, goddesses, and other nonsense. But I did not. I haven't been fooled into thinking that A.A. publishers have abandoned their secularization, revisionism, and universalization; but it may just be that more of the A.A. members who provide the stories are waking up to the sickness involved in referring to Almighty God as a light bulb, a radiator, or "Her."

I certainly don't appreciate the continual running of New York printing presses that causes a proliferation of revised, reprinted, new, and extensive official A.A. literature. Granted, this makes money for A.A. and its staffers if that is anyone's intent now that the enormous royalties to Bill Wilson and family are diminishing. The printing-press philosophy opens the door to more creative idolatry as the anti-God movement grows in America. It adds nothing to saving lives, defining God's will, serving God, loving others, or carrying an agreed message of success.

To be fair, however, I saw far more of God in the new Fourth Edition stories than I've seen in the stuff being cranked out by the A.A. hierarchy in other literature today. Perhaps some of the membership itself is waking up to God, waking up to early A.A. history, waking up to the need for cures rather than more literature, and waking up to the absurdity that has poured and pushed its way into A.A. for the last twenty-five years. Sam Shoemaker himself addressed A.A. with three caveats about: (1) Absurd names for God. (2) Self-made religion. (3) Half-baked prayers. Right or wrong, Sam claimed openly before A.A. people at their International Convention that any "spiritual awakening"–currently and still A.A.'s "solution" to alcoholism–requires four things: (1) Conversion. (2) Prayer. (3) Witness. (4) Fellowship. But those requisites are just not all present in A.A. and its "awakenings" today.

Is there any prospect that we will see an end to phony gods, to undefined "spirituality," to self-made religion, to a fractured fellowship where Christians are trounced and psychobabble is exalted? Possibly the membership itself will awaken to the thump thump thump by those marching out of A.A. Will awaken to the easily observed low success rates of today. Will awaken to the diminishing appeal of meat market meetings. And will awaken to the destructive and unhelpful psychological stuff and the anti-religious dumping at meetings. Possibly more will begin remembering "God" bless America. Possibly more will recall "One nation under God." Possibly some will remember what we old vets heard a few wars back: "Praise the Lord. And pass the ammunition" with the priest, minister, and rabbi rolling up their sleeves for the common endeavor. Possibly some will see the re-runs of Moses, Heston, and even "Jesus Christ Super Star." Just maybe.

I've been surprised and disappointed to see that most of the guys I sponsored a few years back are more and more returning to booze, drugs, and dishonesty. They don't participate in A.A. They don't participate in religious fellowships. They don't stay happy or married or employed. But happily, there are others who offer a benign counterpart.

The guys who were barely in their twenties a few years back are, in some cases, racking up ten to eighteen plus years of sobriety. They have jobs, families, wholesome activities, and a solid relationship with God. And if that's what's come of hearing a little more of God in and out of A.A. recently, it's sure glorifying God. There's much more to pray for, however, if, as I do, you have an interest in, and thankfulness for A.A. Prayer for: (1) More information on early A.A. history. (2) More information on the early reliance on the Creator. (3) More information on the success of the pioneer Christian fellowship–whether you like Christianity or not. (4) More information about the Bible's central role in early A.A. (5) Obliteration of the stupid names given to idols by atheists, agnostics, skeptics, critics, and blow-hards. For such people, Dr. Bob had a simple comment: "I feel sorry for you." He felt sorry for such doubters because they would miss the boat, stay sick, and enrich their ignorance (See the last page of Dr. Bob's personal story in *Alcoholics Anonymous*, 4th ed., p. 181).

Early A.A. did not appeal to the stupid. It appealed to the desperate. It attracted seemingly hopeless, medically incurable people. It offered them God. And God healed and cured them. That assured potential for complete wellness is always still available; and many in today's A.A. are trying to bring the "God medicine" to the fore again and see it work just as it did in the years following 1934. I'm all for it! There's no mass movement to return A.A. to a Christian Fellowship. But there is growing interest in learning what it was like in those early days and just what it demanded and accomplished.

# 6

# The Bible and Alcoholics Anonymous

## The Overview

### Yahweh, the Creator of the Heavens and the Earth

I have written extensively about the Creator in several books and articles on early A.A. See particularly Dick B., *Turning Point: A History of Early A.A.'s Spiritual Roots and Successes*; *Why Early A.A. Succeeded: The Good Book in A.A. Yesterday and Today;* and Appendix 1 of this title.

These writings have seemed imperative because so many are "creating" phony "gods" especially tailored for sick alcoholics and addicts. This tragedy needs to be highlighted, underlined, and repeated often today.

At A.A.'s beginnings, the persuasive language about the Creator came from the Bible itself–A.A.'s only "basic text." It came also from book after book about the Bible that the pioneers read. It came from the devotionals they used in their quiet times. Without exception, these sources told the newcomers what to study, what to learn, and what there was to know about Almighty God, His son Jesus Christ, the gift of the Holy Spirit, the Bible itself, and so many other critical truths. Truths about rescue, forgiveness, healing, loving kindness, and mercy–truths so much needed to be heard by the desperate drinkers.

There is no early history reporting that these pioneer alcoholics were seeking idols, finding strange gods, knocking on the door of New Age philosophy, or establishing new religions, sects, creeds, denominations, or churches. They were urged to go where they had been and renew what they had already learned!

Christian Endeavor–which exerted a strong influence on Dr. Bob in his youth–was, of course, Christian. The churches which continued to be a part of Dr. Bob's life–Congregational, Episcopal, Presbyterian–were, of course, also Christian. The devotionals used by early A.A. people–*The*

*Upper Room, The Runner's Bible, My Utmost for His Highest, The Greatest Thing in the World, Daily Strength for Daily Needs, The Meaning of Prayer, The Imitation of Christ*–were Christian in their message.

God was not shelved in early A.A. He was "found," "explained," and "known."

To contrast this with the nonsense gods of recovery, we have, in writing after writing, devoted much to discussion of Yahweh, our God, the Creator. We have urged and urge greater knowledge and understanding of God's personal name–Yahweh–with the firm belief that when you know His personal name, His titles in the Bible, and His personal attributes, you will not be confused about His identity. You will pay little, if any attention, to some one else's devotion to some "god" of unknown nature or power. You will not sacrifice the lives of desperately sick people who need your help and God's help.

For these reasons, if for no others, the study of the Good Book was, and should be, vital to the recovery and cure of those who believe Dr. Bob: "Your Heavenly Father will never let you down." Vital for those who choose the power of Almighty God as their refuge. For such people, accurate knowledge and understanding of Yahweh are far from impossible. Such knowledge and understanding are critical.

**Three Bible Segments Dr. Bob and the Old-timers Considered "Absolutely Essential"**

I believe a careful reading, understanding, and knowledge of Matthew chapters 5-7, the Book of James, and 1 Corinthians 13 will put the lie to the false notion that early A.A. pioneers were "flying blind" and endured a "flying blind period." Actually, they were being cured.

We urge careful reading of the three segments. Each of these "absolutely essential" portions of the Bible will provide rich descriptions and enable far better understanding of the Akron recovery program, and even the Big Book and Twelve Steps Bill subsequently developed.

You will know that God is God. You will know that love of God and of your neighbor are fundamental principles in A.A. You will realize the significance of worshiping God, serving God, praying to God, and "doing" His word, instead of merely hearing it. You will know that asking

God's guidance, avoiding temptation, helping others, and eliminating anger and grudges, do not involve phony gods, phony principles, or phony self-made religion.. By careful study of the three segments, you can have a clear understanding of our "Heavenly Father," God's love, God's will, God's healing power, God's forgiveness, and living God's law of love.

For a direct focus on the three parts that Dr. Bob called fundamental, see my latest title, *The James Club*, which reviews the picture in detail. Also the Fourth Edition of my latest title *The James Club and The Original A.A. Program's Absolutes Essentials*

**Additional Portions of the Bible the Pioneers Studied**

God is.

> That's what Bill Wilson wrote. That's what Sam Shoemaker wrote. That's what the Bible says in Hebrews 11:6 and Genesis 1:1

God loves. So says John 3:16. God is love. So say 1 John 4:8, 16.

God forgives, heals, and delivers. So says Psalm 103.

God says we should trust Him and acknowledge Him in all our ways. So says Proverbs 3:5-6.

And all these verses were frequently before Akron pioneers.

God tells us very plainly what He made available to every believer through what was accomplished by His son's crucifixion, burial for three days and nights, being raised by God from the dead, and ascending to heaven where Jesus is seated at the right hand of God. The Gospels that Anne recommended tell the facts. The Book of Acts describes the culmination.

God has made salvation available to those who simply make a confession with their mouth and affirm in their heart a simple belief. So says Romans 10:9.

Daily study of Scripture, as urged in Akron and by Dr. Bob and his wife Anne, spreads before the student and believer the promises, commandments, releases, and deliverance that comes only from the

Almighty. It's a big deal. And no one in the early A.A. fellowship doubted it once they accepted Christ.

### A Different Scene Today

Today's treatment programs seldom offer to in-patients, out-patients, after-care, or therapy attendees anything like what the Bible-oriented early A.A. made available. The "treatments" have no power to bring deliverance to the guilty, the fearful, or the sick. And I am witness to the fact that their greatest long-term stress is on not drinking and going to meetings–the more meetings the better, they told me.

Not drinking was a given in early A.A. It was the starting point. It was the *sine qua non.*

Abstinence is how it began. There were infrequent "meetings." Bible study was urged. Fellowship with like-minded believers was urged. Christian living was urged. Prayer was urged. Witnessing was urged.

All these early prescriptions were summed up by Rev. Sam Shoemaker in many of his writings and before A.A. people themselves at their International Convention. Pointing to the A.A. "solution" in a so-called spiritual awakening, Sam said a spiritual awakening involved four things: (1) Conversion. (2) Prayer. (3) Fellowship. (4) Witness. Yet where are they today? The four points were uttered prior to the 1960's and when Bill's "co-founder" Sam Shoemaker was still alive. The four have all but disappeared as a part of A.A.'s "spiritual awakenings."

The scene is different today, and we will let you discern the difference. Our mission is simply to tell it like it was so that you may choose, if you wish, to apply it and live it today.

## A Study of the Sermon on the Mount in A.A. (Matthew Chapters 5-7)

This discussion will not deal with a particular book or commentary on Matthew chapters 5-7. It will focus on the Sermon on the Mount itself; for this Sermon, which Jesus delivered, was not the property of some present-day commentator or writer. The fact that Dr. Bob read the Matthew chapters *themselves,* as well as many interpretations of them, verifies the A.A. belief that the Sermon was one of the principles comprising "the common property of mankind," which Bill Wilson said the AAs had borrowed. And here are some major points that appear to have found their way from the Sermon into the basic ideas of the Big Book. The points were, of course, in the sermon itself. In addition, the pioneers read many books and articles on and about the sermon which are thoroughly documented in the author's title, *The Good Book and The Big Book: A.A.'s Roots in the Bible.* Those items further illustrate some of the points made in the sermon and that might have found their way into A.A.

**The Lord's Prayer—Matthew 6:9-13**

Oxford Group meetings closed with the Lord's Prayer in New York and in Akron. In early A.A., the alcoholics also closed meetings with the Lord's Prayer. Moreover, the author has attended at least two thousand A.A. meetings, and almost every one has closed with the Lord's Prayer. At the 1990 International A.A. Conference in Seattle, which was a first for this author, some 50,000 members of Alcoholics Anonymous joined in closing their meetings with the Lord's Prayer. The question here concerns what parts, if any, of the Lord's Prayer found their way into the Big Book, Twelve Steps, A.A. Slogans, and the A.A. fellowship; and we hasten to remind the reader that the prayer is *part of the Sermon on the Mount.* Here are the verses of the Lord's Prayer (*King James Version*) as found in Matt. 6:9-13. Jesus instructed the Judaeans, "After this manner therefore pray ye":

> Our Father which art in heaven, Hallowed be thy name.
> Thy kingdom come. Thy will be done in earth, as *it is* in heaven. Give us this day our daily bread.
> And forgive us our debts, as we forgive our debtors.
> And lead us not into temptation, but deliver us from evil: For thine is the kingdom, and the power, and the glory, for ever. Amen.

Dr. Bob studied specific commentaries on the Sermon by Oswald Chambers, Glenn Clark, Emmet Fox, and E. Stanley Jones. And these writers extracted a good many teachings, prayer guides, and theological ideas from Lord's Prayer verses in the Sermon. But there are a few concepts and phrases in the Lord's Prayer itself which either epitomize A.A. thinking or can be found in its language—whether the A.A. traces came from the Lord's Prayer or from other portions of the Bible. For example, the Big Book uses the word "Father" when referring to the Creator Yahweh, our God; and the context shows that this usage and name came from the Bible. The Oxford Group also used the term

"Father," among other names, when referring to God. The concept and expression of God as "Father" is not confined to the Sermon on the Mount. It can be found in many other parts of the New Testament. But AAs have given the "Our Father" prayer a special place in their meetings. Thus the Lord's Prayer seems the likely source of their use of the word "Father."

The phrase "Thy will be done" is directly quoted, or is the specific subject of reference, in the Big Book several times (Big Book, 4th ed., pp. 63, 67, 76, 85, 88). It underlies A.A.'s contrast between "self-will" and "God's will." The Oxford Group stressed, as do A.A.'s Third and Seventh Step prayers, that there must be a *decision to do God's will and surrender to His will.* These ideas were also symbolized in the A.A. prayer's "Thy will be done."

Finally, "Forgive us our debts" or "trespasses" certainly states that God can and will "forgive;" and these concepts can be found in the Big Book, whether they came from the Lord's Prayer or from other important Biblical sources such as the Book of James.

**The Full "Sermon on the Mount": Matthew Chapters 5-7**

Dr. Bob studied, and circulated among early AAs, an E. Stanley Jones book, *The Christ of the Mount* (Nashville: Abingdon, 1931; Festival ed., 1985, pp. 36-37) which outlined the Sermon's contents in this fashion:

1. The goal of life: To be perfect or complete as the Father in heaven is perfect or complete (5:48); with twenty-seven marks of this perfect life (5:1-47).

   [Jones wrote of these verses:] The perfect life consists in being poor in spirit, in mourning, in being meek, in hungering and thirsting after righteousness, in being merciful, pure in heart, in being a peacemaker, persecuted for righteousness sake and yet rejoicing and being exceeding glad, in being the salt of the earth, the light of the world, having a righteousness that exceeds, in being devoid of anger with the brother, using no contemptuous words, allowing no one to hold anything against one, having the spirit of quick agreement, no inward lustful thinking, relentless against anything that offends against the highest, right relations in the home life, truth in speech and attitude, turning the other cheek, giving the cloak also, going the second mile, giving to those who ask and from those who would borrow turning not away, loving even one's enemies, praying for those that persecute (pp. 50-51).

2. A diagnosis of the reason why men do not reach or move on to that goal: Divided personality (6:1-6; 7:1-6).

3. The Divine offer of an adequate moral and spiritual re-enforcement so that men can move on to that goal: The Holy Spirit to them that ask him (7:7-11).

4. After making the Divine offer he gathers up and emphasizes in two sentences our part in reaching that goal. Toward others we are to do unto others as we would that they should do unto us (7:12); toward ourselves—we are to lose ourselves by entering the straight gate (7:13).

5. The test of whether we are moving on to that goal, or whether this Divine Life is operative within us: By their fruits (7:15-23).

6. The survival value of this new life and the lack of survival value of life lived in any other way: The house founded on rock and the house founded on sand (7:24-27).

Our own discussion will review Jesus's Sermon, chapter by chapter. It will pinpoint some principal thoughts that Dr. Bob and Bill may have had in mind when they each said that the sermon on the mount contained the underlying philosophy of Alcoholics Anonymous. Here follows our review:

**Matthew Chapter 5**

1. **The Beatitudes**. The Beatitudes are found in Matt. 5:3-11. The word "beatitudes" refers to the first word "Blessed" in each of these verses. Merriam Webster's says "blessed" means "enjoying the bliss of heaven." The word in the Greek New Testament from which "blessed" was translated means, "happy," according Biblical scholar Ethelbert Bullinger. *Vine's Expository Dictionary of Old and New Testament Words* explains the word "Blessed" as follows: "In the beatitudes the Lord

indicates not only the characters that are blessed, but the nature of that which is the highest good." Dr. Bob's wife Anne Smith described the Beatitudes in the Sermon on the Mount as "the Christ-like virtues to be cultivated" (Dick B., *Anne Smith 's Journal,* p. 135).

The beatitude verses can be found at the very beginning of Jesus's sermon and read as follows:

> And seeing the multitudes, he went up into a mountain: and when he was set, his disciples came unto him:
> And he opened his mouth, and taught them, saying,
> Blessed are the poor in spirit: for theirs is the kingdom of heaven.
> Blessed are they that mourn: for they shall be comforted.
> Blessed are the meek: for they shall inherit the earth.
> Blessed are they which do hunger and thirst after righteousness: for they shall be filled.
> Blessed are the merciful: for they shall obtain mercy.
> Blessed are the pure in heart: for they shall see God.
> Blessed are the peacemakers: for they shall be called the children of God.
> Blessed are they which are persecuted for righteousness' sake: for theirs is the kingdom of heaven.
> Blessed are ye, when men shall revile you, and persecute you, and shall say all manner of evil against you falsely, for my sake.
> Rejoice, and be exceeding glad: for great is your reward in heaven: for so persecuted they the prophets which were before you (Matt. 5:1-12)

Italicized below are *Webster's* definitions for the key words in each "beatitude" verse, with quotes also from the *King James Version*, which was the version Dr. Bob and early AAs most used. As the verses appear in the King James, they state: "Blessed" are:

- the poor *(humble)* in spirit [renouncing themselves, wrote E. Stanley Jones]: for theirs is the kingdom of heaven (v. 3) ;
- they that mourn *(feel or express grief or sorrow):* for they shall be comforted (v. 4);
- the meek *(enduring injury with patience and without resentment);* for they shall inherit the earth (v. 5);
- they which do hunger and thirst after righteousness *(acting in accord with divine or moral law):* for they shall be filled (v. 6);
- the merciful *(compassionate):* for they shall obtain mercy (v. 7);
- the pure *(spotless, stainless)* in heart [has a passion for righteousness and a compassion for men–seeks law and shows love, wrote Jones]: for they shall see God (v. 8);

- the peacemakers: for they shall be called the children of God (v. 9);
- they which are persecuted for righteousness sake: for theirs is the kingdom of heaven (v. 10);
- ye when men shall revile you, and persecute you, and shall say all manner of evil against you falsely, for my sake *(end or purpose):* for great is your reward in heaven: for so persecuted they the prophets which were before you (v. 11).

Did Dr. Bob, Anne, Bill, or Henrietta Seiberling study and draw specifically on these beatitude verses as they put together A.A.'s recovery program? The author can neither provide nor document any answer. But there are some ideas common to A.A.'s spiritual principles in the beatitudes as you see them expressed above. These are: (1) Humility–overcoming self; (2) Comfort for the suffering; (3) Patience and tolerance to the end of eliminating resentment; (4) Harmonizing one's actions with God's will; (5) Compassion, which *Webster* defines as "sympathetic consciousness of others distress together with a desire to alleviate;" (6) "Cleaning house"–which means seeking obedience to God and, based on the principles of love, straightening out harms caused by disobedience; (7) Making peace; (8) Standing for and acting upon spiritual principles, whatever the cost, because they are God's principles. The foregoing are Twelve Step ideas that can be found in the Beatitudes; and A.A. founders probably saw them there as well, and they can most certainly be found in the Big Book–humility, comforting others, patience and tolerance, "Thy will be done," compassion, amends, peacemaking, acting on the "cardinal principles of Jesus Christ" as virtues to be cultivated.

2. **Letting your light shine**. Matt. 5:13-16 suggest glorifying your Heavenly Father by letting others *see* your good works. That is, "Letting your light shine" does not mean glorifying yourself, but rather glorifying God by letting others see your spiritual walk *in action*—to see the immediate results of your surrender to the Master. These ideas may be reflected in the Big Book's statement: "Our real purpose is to fit ourselves to be of maximum service to God. . . ." (p. 77).

3. **Obeying the Ten Commandments**. In Matt. 5:17-21, Jesus reiterates the importance of obeying the law and the prophets, specifically referring to Exod. 20:13 (Thou shalt not kill), but obviously referring to the other important commandments such as having no other god but Yahweh (Exod. 20:2-3), worshiping no other god (Exod. 20:4-5),

eschewing adultery (Exod. 20:14), not stealing (Exod. 20:15), and so on. And even though some of these commandments may have fallen between the cracks in today's A.A., they very clearly governed the moral standards of early A.A. that Dr. Bob and the Akron AAs embraced. The Ten Commandments were part of early A.A. pamphlets and literature, and (for example) Dr. Bob and the Akron AAs would have nothing to do with a man who was committing adultery.

4. **The Law of Love in action**. In Matt. 5:17-47, Jesus confirms that the Law of Love fulfills the Old Testament Law. He rejects anger without cause, unresolved wrongs to a brother, quibbling with an adversary, lust and impurity, adultery, retaliation, and hatred of an enemy. The author's title *The Oxford Group & Alcoholics Anonymous* covers many of these ideas as roots of A.A. principles. And the foregoing verses in Matthew may very well have influenced A.A. language about: (1) Overcoming resentments [". . .I say unto you, That whosoever is angry with his brother without a cause shall be in danger of the judgment. . .]; (2) Making restitution ["Therefore if thou bring thy gift before the altar, and there rememberest that thy brother hath ought against thee; Leave there thy gift before the altar, and go thy way; first be reconciled to thy brother, and then come and offer thy gift"]; (3) Avoidance of retaliation for wrongdoing by others ["Ye have heard that it hath been said, An eye for an eye, and a tooth for a tooth: But I say unto you, That ye resist not evil: but whosoever shall smite thee on thy right cheek, turn to him the other also"]; and (4) Making peace with our enemies ["Ye have heard that it hath been said, Thou shalt love thy neighbor, and hate thine enemy. But I say unto you. Love your enemies, bless them that curse you, do good to them that hate you, and pray for them which despitefully use you, and persecute you"]

## Matthew Chapter 6

1. **Anonymity**. Matt. 6:1-8, 16-18 (urging almsgiving "in secret," praying "in secret," fasting "in secret," and avoiding "vain repetitions," and hypocrisy) very possibly played a role in the development of A.A.'s spiritual principle of anonymity. Jesus said, "your Father knoweth what things ye have need of, before ye ask him" and "thy Father, which seeth in secret. shall reward thee openly." The vain practices which Jesus condemned were focused on one's inflating the ego and focus on self-centeredness--something A.A. disdains. Early Oxford Group and A.A. literature often spoke of "God-sufficiency" versus "self-sufficiency," and "God-centeredness" versus "self-centeredness" and "ego-centricity." We

have located no direct tie between the teachings of Jesus on anonymity and A.A.'s traditions on this "spiritual" principle. But the concepts are parallel; and *The Runner's Bible* and other A.A. biblical sources that AAs studied do discuss their significance at some length.

2. **Forgiveness**. Matt. 6:14-15 refer to forgiving men their trespasses; and Emmet Fox's forceful writing about these verses may well have influenced the A.A. amends process. Fox said:

> The forgiveness of sins is the central problem of life. . . . It is, of course, rooted in selfishness. . . . We must positively and definitely extend forgiveness to everyone to whom it is possible that we can owe forgiveness, namely, to anyone who we think can have injured us in any way. . . When you hold resentment against anyone, you are bound to that person by a cosmic link, a real, tough metal chain. You are tied by a cosmic tie to the thing that you hate. The one person perhaps in the whole world whom you most dislike is the very one to whom you are attaching yourself by a hook that is stronger than steel (Fox, *The Sermon on the Mount,* pp. 183-88).

There is no assurance that Fox's writing on this sermon's forgiveness point specifically influenced the Big Book's emphasis on forgiveness. To be sure, at least two A.A. history writers have claimed that Fox's writings did influence Bill Wilson. However, other books that were read by early AAs–books by such authors as Henry Drummond, Glenn Clark, E. Stanley Jones, and Harry Emerson Fosdick–used language similar to that used by Fox in his discussion of forgiveness of enemies. And Jesus' sermon on the mount is not the only place in the New Testament where forgiveness is stressed. Thus, after, and even though, Christ had accomplished remission of past sins of believers, Paul wrote:

> Forbearing one another, and forgiving one another, if any man have a quarrel against any: even as Christ forgave you, so also *do ye* (Col. 3:13)

See also the following verse, a favorite often quoted and used by Henrietta Seiberling–a well known early A.A. teacher who was often thought of as an A.A. founder:

> If a man say I love God, and hateth his brother. he is a liar: for he that loveth not his brother whom he hath seen, how can he love God whom he hath not seen? (1 John 4:20)

In any event, the Big Book, Fourth Edition, states at page 77:

> The question of how to approach the man we hated will arise. It may be he has done us more harm than we have done him and, though we may have acquired a better attitude toward him, we are still not too keen about admitting our faults. Nevertheless, with a person we dislike, we take the bit in our teeth. It is harder to go to an enemy than to a friend, but we find it more beneficial to us. We go to him in a helpful *and forgiving spirit,* confessing our former ill feeling and expressing our regret. Under no condition do we criticize such a person or argue. Simply we tell him that we will never get over drinking until we have done our utmost to straighten out the past (italics added).

3. **"The sunlight of the Spirit?"** Speaking of the futility and unhappiness in a life which includes deep resentment, the Big Book states: "when harboring such feelings we shut ourselves off from the sunlight of the Spirit." One often hears this "sunlight" expression quoted in A.A. meetings. Yet its origins seem unreported and undocumented. Anne Smith referred frequently in her journal to the verses in 1 John which had to do with fellowship with God and walking in the light as God is light. So did A.A.'s Oxford Group sources. And the following are the most frequently quoted verses from 1 John having to do with God as "light" and the importance of walking in the light (rather than walking in darkness) in order to have fellowship with Him:

> That which we have seen and heard declare we unto you, that ye may have fellowship with us: and truly our fellowship *is* with the Father, and with his Son, Jesus Christ.
> And these things write we unto you, that your joy may be full.
> This then is the message which we have heard of him, and declare unto you, that God is light, and in him is no darkness at all.
> If we say that we have fellowship with him, and walk in darkness, we lie, and do not the truth:
> But if we walk in the light, as he is in the light, we have fellowship one with another, and the blood of Jesus Christ his Son cleanseth us from all sin (1 John 1:3-7).

Though this particular discussion is concerned with the Sermon on the Mount, we have mentioned also the foregoing verses from 1 John 1:3-7 (having to do with walking in God's light as against opposed to walking in darkness). For very possibly those ideas in 1 John, together with the following verses in the Sermon, may have given rise to Bill's references to the alcoholic's being blocked from the "sunlight of the Spirit" when he or she dwells in such dark realms as excessive anger. Matt. 6:22-24 (in the Sermon) state:

> The light of the body is the eye: if therefore thine eye be single, thy whole body shall be full of light.
> But if thine eye be evil, thy whole body shall be full of darkness. If therefore the light that is in thee be darkness, how great *is* that darkness!
> No man can serve two masters: for either he will hate the one, and love the other: or else he will hold to the one, and despise the other. Ye cannot serve God and mammon.

4. **Seek ye first the kingdom of God**. Matt. 6:24-34 seem to have had tremendous influence on A.A. The substance of these verses is that man will be taken care of when he seeks *first* the kingdom of God and His righteousness. Verse 33 says:

> But seek ye first the kingdom of God, and his righteousness; and all these things [food. clothing, and shelter] shall be added unto you.

Dr. Bob specifically explained the origin of our A.A. slogans "Easy Does It" and "First Things First." *(DR.* BOB *and the Good Oldtimers,* pp 135, 144). When he was asked the meaning of "First Things First," Dr. Bob replied. "Seek ye first the kingdom of God and His righteousness, and all these things shall be added unto you." He told his sponsee Clarence S. that "First Things First" came from Matt. 6:33 in the sermon on the mount. And this verse was widely quoted in the books that Dr. Bob and the Akron AAs read and recommended (Dick B., *The Good Book and The Big Book,* p. 125, n.119; *That Amazing Grace*, pp. 30, 38).

On page 60, the Big Book states the A.A. solution for relief from alcoholism: "God could and would if He were sought." This concept of "seeking" results by reliance on God instead of reliance on self is a bedrock idea in the Big Book (see Third Edition, pp. 11, 14, 25, 28, 43, 52-53, 57, 62). In view of Dr. Bob's explanations as to the origin of "First Things First," the Big Book's emphasis on "seeking" very likely came from the "seeking the kingdom of God first" idea in Matt. 6:33.

According to Dr. Bob, the slogans "Easy Does It" and "One day at a time" came from the next verse–Matthew 6:34. See Dick B., *The Good Book and The Big Book*, pp. 87-88, and other citations therein.

**Matthew Chapter 7**

1. **Taking your own inventory**. Much of A.A.'s Fourth, Ninth, Tenth, and Eleventh Step actions involve looking for your own part, for your own fault in troublesome matters. This self-examination process (as part of the house-cleaning and life-changing process in the Steps) was expected to result in that which, in Appendix II of the Third Edition of the Big Book, became described as "the personality change sufficient to bring about recovery from alcoholism" (Big Book, p. 569). Matt. 7:3-5 states:

> And why beholdest thou the mote [speck] that is in thy brother's eye, but considerest not the beam [log] that is in thine own eye?
> Or how wilt thou say to thy brother, Let me pull the mote [speck] out of thine eye; and, behold, a beam [log] *is* in thine own eye.
> Thou hypocrite, first cast out the beam [log] out of thine own eye; and then shalt thou see clearly to cast out the mote [speck] out of thy brother's eye.

These verses from Matthew were frequently cited by A.A.'s spiritual sources as the Biblical foundation for self-examination and thus finding one's own part, one's own erroneous conduct, in a relationship problem.

2. **Ask, seek, knock**. Matt. 7:7-11 states:

> Ask, and it shall be given you; seek, and ye shall find; knock, and it shall be opened unto you;
> For every one that asketh receiveth; and he that seeketh findeth; and to him that knocketh it shall be opened.
> Or what man is there of you, whom if his son ask bread, will he give him a stone? Or if he ask a fish, will he give him a serpent?
> If ye then, being evil, know how to give good gifts unto your children, how much more shall your Father which is in heaven give good things to them that ask him?

Bill Wilson's spiritual teacher, Rev. Sam Shoemaker, wrote:

> Our part [in the crisis of self-surrender] is to ask, to seek, to knock. His [God's] part is to answer, to come, to open (Shoemaker, *Realizing Religion,* p. 32).

*The Runner's Bible* (one of the most important of the early A.A. Bible devotionals) has an entire chapter titled, "Ask and Ye shall receive." Another favored devotional among the A.A. pioneers was *My Utmost for His Highest,* by Oswald Chambers. Chambers says, about the foregoing verses beginning with Matt. 7:7:

> The illustration of prayer that Our Lord uses here is that of a good child asking for a good thing. . . . It is no use praying unless we are living as children of God. Then, Jesus says: "Everyone that asketh receiveth."

The foregoing verses, and relevant comments by A.A. sources, underline the importance of becoming a child of God, establishing a harmonious relationship with Him, and *then* expecting good results from the Creator, Yahweh, our God–"Providence" from Him as our Heavenly Father. Given the emphasis in early A.A. on the Sermon, those verses from Matt. 7 very probably influenced the following similar ideas expressed as follows in the Big Book's Third Edition and Fourth Edition:

> If what we have learned and felt and seen means anything at all, it means that all of us, whatever our race, creed, or color are the children of a living Creator with whom we may form a relationship upon simple and understandable terms as soon as we are willing and honest enough to try (p. 28).

> God will constantly disclose more to you and to us. Ask Him in your morning meditation what you can do each day for the man who is still sick. The answers will come, *if your own house is in order.* But obviously you cannot transmit something you haven't got. See *to it that your relationship with Him is right,* and great events will come to pass for you and countless others. This is the Great Fact for us (p. 164, italics added).

In this same vein. Dr. Bob's wife, Anne, wrote, in the spiritual journal she shared with early AAs and their families:

> We can't give away what we haven't got. We must have a genuine contact with God in our present experience. Not an experience of the past, but an experience in the present—actual, genuine (Dick B., *Anne Smith's Journal*, p. 121).

3. **Do unto others**. The so-called "Golden Rule" cannot, as such, be readily identified in A.A.'s Big Book though it certainly is a much-quoted portion of the sermon on the mount which Bill and Dr. Bob said underlies A.A.'s philosophy. The relevant verse is Matt. 7:12:

> Therefore all things whatsoever ye would that men should do to you, do ye even so to them: for this is the law and the prophets.

Perhaps the following two Big Book segments bespeak that philosophy as Bill may have seen it:

> We have begun to learn tolerance, patience and good will toward all men, even our enemies, for we look on them as sick people. We have listed the people we have hurt by our conduct, and are willing to straighten out the past if we can (p. 70).

> Then you will know what it means to give of yourself that others may survive and rediscover life. You will learn the full meaning of "Love thy neighbor as thyself" (p. 153).

4. **He that doeth the will of my Father**. There are *several* key verses in the sermon on the mount which could have caused Bob and Bill to say that Matthew Chapters Five to Seven contained A.A.'s underlying philosophy. The verses are in the Lords Prayer itself (Matt. 6:9-13), the so-called Golden Rule quoted above (Matt. 7:12), and the phrase "Thy will be done" (Matt. 6:10). In addition to these three roots, however, I believe that the major spiritual principle borrowed by the founders from the sermon on the mount—can be found in Matt. 7:21:

> Not every one that saith unto me. Lord, Lord, shall enter into the kingdom of heaven; but he that doeth the will of my Father which is in heaven.

Bill Wilson said clearly in the Big Book and in his other writings that the key to success in A.A. is doing the will of the Father–the Father Who is the *subject* of the Lord's Prayer, Almighty God Whose will was to be done, and the Creator upon whom early AAs relied. Note that Wilson wrote:

> I was to sit quietly when in doubt, asking only for direction and strength to meet my problems as He would have me (Bill's Story, Big Book, 4th ed., p. 13).

He humbly offered himself to his Maker—then he knew (Big Book, 4th ed., p. 57).

. . . praying only for knowledge of His will for us and the power to carry that out (Step Eleven, Big Book, 4th ed., p. 59).

May I do Thy will always (portion of "Third Step Prayer," Big Book, 4th ed., p. 63)!

Thy will be done (Big Book, 4th ed, pp. 67, 88).

Grant me strength, as I go out from here, to do your bidding. Amen (portion of "Seventh Step Prayer," Big Book, 4th ed., p. 76).

There is God, our Father, who very simply says, 'I am waiting for you to do my will' *(Alcoholics Anonymous Comes of Age,* p. 105).

## A Study of the Book of James in A.A.

Of probably even greater importance (than the Sermon) in the day-by-day thinking of early A.A. was the Book of James. It was much studied by A.A.'s co-founders. Quotes and ideas from the Apostle James can be found throughout the Big Book and in A.A. literature. The Book of James was considered so important that many favored calling the A.A. fellowship the "James Club" *(DR. BOB and the Good Oldtimers,* p. 71; *Pass It On,* p. 147). And even the most fundamental phrases in A.A., such as "It Works" and Bill Wilson's own "Works Publishing Company" (which published the First Edition of the Big Book), probably have their origin in the "Faith without works is dead" phrases in the Book of James (See: Nell Wing, *Grateful to Have Been There,* pp. 70-71).

Let's therefore review the Book of James, chapter by chapter. As we do so, we will point to traces of that book which we believe can be found in, or probably influenced the text of, the Big Book. At the outset, we would report that as our research into the Biblical roots of A.A. has progressed, so has our understanding of some root sources that previously went unnoticed.

For example, some time back, Dr. Bob's son, Robert R. Smith, told the author by phone that his father had placed great stake in *The Runner's Bible.* We had encountered difficulty locating a copy. And we were still looking for some commentary on the Book of James similar to the many on the sermon on the mount (by Oswald Chambers, Glenn Clark, Emmet Fox, and E. Stanley Jones) and on 1 Corinthians 13 (by Henry Drummond, for example). And Dr. Bob extensively studied and circulated most of these among the Pioneers. We believed such above-mentioned commentaries probably impacted upon the thinking of Dr. Bob, Anne, Henrietta, and the early AAs just as the actual Bible verses in Matthew chapters 5-7 and 1 Corinthians 13 have.

But we could find no similar commentary that the pioneers used with the Book of James, despite A.A.'s specific emphasis on James. Finally, as we studied the spiritual literature early AAs read, we noticed in *The Runner's Bible* the frequency with which all the books and chapters that Dr. Bob called "absolutely essential" (Matthew chapters 5-7, 1 Corinthians 13, and James) were there mentioned. We particularly noticed the frequency with which *The Runner's Bible* mentioned and discussed verses from the Book of James. Hence our reader will find many references to *The Runner's Bible* in the footnotes of our title *The Good Book and The Big Book;* for we believe that the little "Runner's" devotional book may have provided Dr. Bob, Anne Smith, and perhaps even Bill Wilson, with much of the fodder that caused them to focus on James and conclude that James was their "favorite" book of the Bible.

In a phone conversation with the author in 1995, from his home in Texas, Dr. Bob's son stated he felt it would be almost impossible for him, at this late date, to confirm that *The Runner's Bible* was the source of either A.A.'s or its founders' emphasis on James or other parts of the Bible. But he pointed out that the little Biblical devotional book was used by those who wanted a quick and easy source for Biblical ideas in which they were interested. Perhaps, then, that book became a reference source for Dr. Bob, Anne, and even Bill Wilson when they were studying the pertinent Biblical ideas they extracted from 1 Corinthians 13, the Sermon on the Mount, and particularly James. Now let's look at the chapters in James–one by one.

**James Chapter 1**

1. **Patience**. Chapter One is not the only chapter in the Book of James which mentions patience. Nor is it the only portion of the Bible that stresses patience. But we've noted that James was a favored Biblical source in early A.A., and James 1:3-4 do state:

> Knowing *this,* that the trying of your faith worketh patience. But let patience have *her* perfect work, that ye may be perfect and entire, wanting nothing.

Patience certainly wound up as one of the most frequently mentioned spiritual principles in the Big Book (pp. 67, 70, 83, 111, 118, 163).

2. **Asking wisdom of God with unwavering believing**. James 1:5-8 state:

> If any of you lack wisdom, let him ask of God, that giveth to all *men* liberally, and upbraideth not; and it shall be given him.
> But let him ask in faith, nothing wavering. For he that wavereth is like a wave of the sea driven with the wind and tossed.
> For let not that man think that he shall receive anything of the Lord. A double minded man *is* unstable in all his ways.

Asking for God's direction and strength and receiving "Guidance" from Him, are major themes in both the Old and New Testaments. They were important Oxford Group ideas as well. We therefore discussed them at length in our titles on the Oxford Group and on Anne Smith's spiritual journal. Certainly the Big Book, including the Eleventh Step itself, is filled with such Guidance concepts (3rd ed., pp.13, 46, 49, 62-63, 69-70, 76, 79-80, 83, 84-88, 100, 117, 120, 124, 158, 164).

3. **Resisting temptation**. It should surprise no one that AAs of yesteryear and of today are interested in resisting temptation, and having the power to do that—the power of God. James 1:12-16 state:

> Blessed *is* the man that endureth temptation: for when he is tried, he shall receive the crown of life, which the Lord hath promised to those that love him.
> Let no man say when he is tempted, I am tempted of God: for God cannot be tempted with evil, neither tempteth he any man:
> But every man is tempted when he is drawn away of his own lust and enticed.
> Then when lust bath conceived, it bringeth forth sin: and sin, when it is finished, bringeth forth death.

Do not err, my beloved brethren.

[My personal view is that the foregoing verses offer much insight into the *cure* of alcoholism and other life-controlling afflictions. Man is to resist the devil–says James in a later verse. Man is to endure temptation when he is tried. When he is tempted, he cannot blame the temptation on God–who cannot be tempted and does not tempt. He can be tempted by being drawn away of his own lust and enticed. James 3:15-16 speaks of a "wisdom [that] descendeth not from above, but is earthly, sensual, and devilish." And, says James, when the enticement results in lustful [and excessive] thoughts and behavior [such as getting drunk and drunkenness], it can and should be recognized as sin, and sin as the producer of death. For the real alcoholic, the devilish thoughts must be expelled. The prescription is not merely to abstain from drinking and go to 12 Step meetings. That's not in the Book of James. The enjoined error occurs when the man fails to submit to God, resist the devil, humble himself in the sight of God, and appropriately believe to be lifted up and out by his Creator. 2 Corinthians 10:5 calls for casting down human reasoning and "every high thing that exalteth itself against the knowledge of God, and bringing into captivity every thought to the obedience of Christ." We are the ones to control the thoughts. 1 Corinthians 10:13 points out: "There hath no temptation taken you but such as is common to man; but God is faithful, who will not suffer you to be tempted above that ye are able; but will with the temptation also make a way to escape, that ye may be able to bear it." To be "cured," I believe, we need to recognize that temptation to disobey God is common, that thoughts about letting the temptation make a nest in our mind and motivate must be cast out. They need to be resisted. They need to be expelled. And we need to believe what God says–we are submit ourselves to God; resist the devil; and be assured that the devil will flee, that God will lift us up, and that we can escape and bear the temptation with the help of our faithful Creator.]

4. **Every good and perfect gift comes from God, the Father of lights.** James 1:17 states:

> Every good gift and every perfect gift is from above, and cometh down from the Father of lights, with whom is no variableness, neither shadow of turning.

Bill seemed to be referring to this verse when he wrote on page 14 of *Alcoholics Anonymous*, 4th ed.:

> I must turn in all things to the Father of Light [sic] who presides over us all. [Alcoholics Anonymous, 1st ed., has "the Father of Lights," p. 23.]

Bill made the same reference to God, the Father of lights, who presides over us all, in Appendix I of *Alcoholics Anonymous*, 4th ed.:

> This to the end that our great blessings may never spoil us; that we shall forever live in thankful contemplation of Him who presides over us all (p. 566).

The "Him" who presides over us all was, of course, James 1:17's "Father of lights"– the Creator Yahweh, our Almighty God.

5. **Let every man be slow to speak, slow to wrath**. James 1:19-20 state:

> Wherefore, my beloved brethren, let every man be swift to hear, slow to speak, slow to wrath: For the wrath of man worketh not the righteousness of God.

The same verse is quoted in *The Runner's Bible* and seems quite relevant to the Big Book's
injunction, "If we were to live, we had to be free of anger. . . . God save me from being angry" (Fourth Edition, pp. 66-67).

6. **Be ye doers of the word, and not hearers only**. James 1:21-22 state:

> Wherefore lay apart all filthiness and superfluity of naughtiness, and receive with meekness the engrafted word, which is able to save your souls.
> But be ye doers of the word, and not hearers only, deceiving your own selves.

Reverend Sam Shoemaker made this comment on the foregoing:

> I think St. James' meaning is made much clearer in Dr. Moffatt's translation, "Act on the Word, instead of merely listening to it." Try it out in experiment, and prove it by its results—otherwise you only fool yourself into believing that you have the heart of religion when you haven't (Shoemaker, *The Gospel According to You,* pp. 44-55).

In the same chapter, Shoemaker also pointed out that prayer is often more a struggle to find God than the enjoyment of Him and cooperation with His will. He added that "God is and is a Rewarder of them that seek Him." (See *The Gospel According to You,* p. 47; and Heb. 11:6).

We cannot find specific or similar language to that of James 1:21-22 in the Big Book; but A.A. declares over and over that A.A. is a program of *action,* that probably no human power can relieve a person of his alcoholism, and "That God could and would if He were *sought"* (p. 60). A.A.'s program emphasizes action in the experiment of faith it adopted from John 7:17—*seeking* God by *following* the path that leads to a relationship with God. James 1:22 enjoins *doing* God's will as expressed in His Word—not merely listening to it. James was an Akron favorite. Shoemaker was a Wilson favorite. "Faith without works" was a Big Book favorite; and it therefore seems quite reasonable to believe and possible that A.A.'s emphasis on *action* might well have derived in part from James 1:21-22.

7. **Pure religion and undefiled before God . . . to visit the fatherless and widows in their affliction**. James 1:27 states:

> Pure religion and undefiled before God and the Father is this, To visit the fatherless and widows in their affliction, *and* to keep oneself unspotted from the world.

At the very least, this verse bespeaks unselfishness and helpfulness to others which were cardinal A.A. principles–particularly the principles embodied in Step Twelve. In fact, that's the point made in one of early A.A.'s pamphlets:

> And all we need to do in the St. James passage is to substitute the word "Alcoholic" for "Fatherless and Widows" and we have Step Twelve (*Spiritual Milestones*, AA of Akron, pp. 12-13).

**James Chapter 2**

Chapter Two of the Book of James may have made two direct and major contributions to the language of the Big Book and also to A.A.'s philosophy. Those two contributions were "Love thy neighbor as thyself" and "Faith without works is dead."

1. **Love thy neighbor as thyself**. James 2:8 states:

> If ye fulfill the royal law according to the scripture, Thou shalt love thy neighbor as thyself, ye do well.

This commandment to "Love thy neighbor" exists in other parts of both the Old and New Testaments. Thus, when the Big Book incorporated this phrase, there is no assurance that the
quote is from James rather than from another Bible verse to the same effect (*e.g.*, Rom. 13:9; Gal. 5:14). But the Big Book certainly does state:

> Then you will know what it means to give of yourself that others may survive and rediscover life. You will learn the full meaning of "Love thy neighbor as thyself" (p. 153).

The Book of James is very probably the specific source of this Biblical quote since Dr. Bob, early AAs, and Bill Wilson himself spoke with such frequency about "love" and tolerance as the code of A.A. *and* the Book of James as their favorite book.

2. **Faith without works is dead**. Said to be the favorite verse of Anne Smith and perhaps the origin of many expressions in A.A. concerning "works," this sentence, or variations of it, appears several times in Chapter Two of the Book of James. For example, James 2:20 states:

> But wilt thou know, 0 vain man, that faith without works is dead?

"Faith without works" as a phrase, and as an A.A. "action" concept, is quoted or referred to many times in the Big Book (4th ed., pp. 14-15, 76, 88, 93, 97). A.A.'s original Oxford Group connection also put emphasis on these James verses, using them in connection with the importance of witnessing. Sometimes I believe that A.A. has put lots of emphasis on "works" and forgotten the "faith part." The "faith" is the faith of Jesus Christ. Galatians 2:16 says:

> Knowing that a man is not justified by the works of the law, but by the faith of Jesus Christ, even we have believed in Jesus Christ, that we might be justified by the faith of Christ, and not by the works of the law: for by the works of the law shall no flesh be justified.

3. **Helping Others**. It hardly requires citation or documentation to state that A.A.'s cardinal objective is to help others. And this service concept is underlined in Chapter 2 of James, beginning with verses 1 to 7. James 2:15-16 state this principle very well:

> If a brother or sister be naked, and destitute of daily food, And one of you say unto them, Depart in peace, be ye warmed and filled; notwithstanding ye give them not those things which are needful to the body; what doth it profit? Even so, faith, if it hath not works, is dead, being alone.

And every alcoholic who has helped one of his miserable, suffering, destitute brothers in need will instantly relate to those verses and hence to the importance of James to the early AAs.

4. **The Ten Commandments. Again!** James 2:10-11 state:

> For whosoever shall keep the whole law, and yet offend in one *point,* he is guilty of all. For he that said, Do not commit adultery, said also, Do not kill. Now if thou commit no adultery, yet if thou kill, thou art become a transgressor of the law.

[Whatever one may find in today's A.A., he will find language about and references to the Ten Commandments with great frequency in *early* A.A. The Frank Amos report of 1938, quoted in this paper, is a good example.]

**James Chapter 3**

1. **Taming the tongue**. In his Farewell Address to A.A., Dr. Bob said:

> Let us also remember to guard that erring member the tongue, and if we must use it, let's use it with kindness and consideration and tolerance *(DR. BOB and the Good Oldtimers,* p. 338).

A major portion of James chapter 3 is devoted to the trouble that can be caused by an untamed tongue. Following are a few verses emphasizing the point:

> Even so the tongue is a little member and boasteth great things. Behold, how great a matter a little fire kindleth! And the tongue *is* a fire, a world of iniquity; so is the tongue among our members that it defileth the whole body, and setteth on fire the course of nature; and *it is* set on fire of hell.
> But the tongue can no man tame; it is an unruly evil, full of deadly poison.
> Out of the same mouth proceedeth blessing and cursing. My brethren, these things ought not to be (James 3:5, 6, 8, 10)

These verses are not quoted in the Big Book. But Anne Smith referred to them frequently in her journal, as did other A.A. roots sources (Dick B., *Anne Smith's Journal,* pp. 28, 44, 76, 77; Holm, *The Runner's Bible,* p. 68). But, in paraphrasing those verses, Dr. Bob seemed to be speaking of the necessity for tolerance, courtesy, consideration, and kindness in our speech and actions. James makes clear that good *conversation* should be a focus—conversation, we believe, that is laced with consideration, kindness, and tolerance (See James 3:13). And these latter principles *are* very much in evidence in the Big Book (4th ed., pp. 67, 69-70, 83-84, 97, 118, 125, 135).

2. **Avoidance of envy, strife, and lying**. James 3:14-16 proclaim that a heart filled with envy, strife, and lies has not received that kind of "wisdom" from God, but rather from devilish sources. The verses state:

> But if ye have bitter envying and strife in your hearts; glory not, and lie not against the truth.
> This wisdom descendeth not from above, but is earthly, sensual, devilish.
> For where envying and strife is, there is confusion and every evil work.

"Envy" is not as much decried in the Big Book as jealousy; but a more modern translation of these King James verses equates "envy" *with* "jealousy" (*The Revised English Bible, New Testament*, p, 208). And the Big Book most assuredly condemns jealously ($4^{th}$ ed., pp. 37, 69, 82, 100, 119, 145, 161). In fact, the Big Book states as to jealousy *and* envy:

> Keep it always in sight that we are dealing with that most terrible human emotion–jealousy (p. 82).

> The greatest enemies of us alcoholics are resentment, jealousy, envy, frustration, and fear (p. 145).

And as to strife, the Big Book states:

> After all, our problems were of our own making. Bottles were only a symbol. Besides, we have stopped fighting anybody or anything. We have to (p. 103)!

James 3:17-18 talk much about making peace and the fruit of righteousness being sown in peace of them that make peace.

As seen in the quote from James 3:14, lying and dishonesty are also declared to be devilish; and one should note and compare the Big Book's frequent emphasis on grasping and developing a manner of living which "demands rigorous honesty" (p. 58). As to all the verses in James 3:14-16, however, there is little certainty that these particular verses were an exclusive or even major source for the Big Book's condemnation of envy, jealousy, strife, and dishonesty because all these traits are stated to be objectionable by many other parts of the Bible.

**James Chapter 4**

1. **Asking amiss for selfish ends**. A.A.'s writings have much to say about overcoming selfishness and self-centeredness. But the following in James 4:3 particularly eschews selfishness in prayer:

Ye ask, and receive not, because ye ask amiss, that ye may consume it upon your lusts.

Several Christian A.A. sources that were favorites of Dr. Bob's discuss this verse at length. And the Big Book authors may therefore have borrowed from James 4:3, in this statement:

We ask especially for freedom from self-will, and are careful to make no request for ourselves only. We may ask for ourselves, however, if others will be helped. We are careful never to pray for our own selfish ends. Many of us have wasted a lot of time doing that and it doesn't work (Big Book, 4th ed., p. 87).

2. **Humility**. The Book of James has no corner on the Biblical injunction to be humble. But the importance of James, and the remarks of Reverend Sam Shoemaker (quoted under Item 3 immediately below) suggest that the following verses from James may have been a source of the Big Book's frequent mention of humility. James 4:7, 10 state:

Submit yourselves therefore to God. Resist the devil, and he will flee from you.
Humble yourselves in the sight of the Lord, and he shall lift you up.

The Big Book's Fourth Edition is filled with exhortations to be humble, with stress on humbling one's self before God, and with suggestions for humbly asking His help. Examples include:

There I humbly offered myself to God, as I understood Him, to do with me as He would (p. 13).

He humbly offered himself to his Maker—then he knew (p. 57).

Just to the extent that we do as we think He would have us, and humbly rely on Him, does He enable us to match calamity with serenity (p. 68).

We constantly remind ourselves we are no longer running the show, humbly saying to ourselves many times each day "Thy will be done" (pp. 87-88).

3. **Trusting God and cleaning house**. James 4:8 states:

> Draw nigh to God, and he will draw nigh to you. Cleanse your hands, ye sinners; and purify your hearts, ye double minded.

The Big Book says on page 98 of the Fourth Edition:

> Burn the idea into the consciousness of every man that he can get well regardless of anyone. The only condition is that he trust in God and clean house.

And, in language closely paralleling that in James 4:8, the Big Book says further that one can establish conscious companionship with God by simply, honestly, and humbly seeking and drawing near to Him:

> He has come to all who have honestly sought Him. When we drew near to Him He disclosed Himself to us (page 57)!

In Step Seven, the Big Book relates "cleaning house" of one's character defects to "humbly asking" God to remove them. The foregoing verses in James, which speak of drawing near to God, cleansing our hearts, humbling ourselves in His sight, and then being "lifted" up by God, appear to have been directly involved in framing the Big Book's Seventh Step language. In fact, many years after the Big Book was written, Sam Shoemaker thus clarified his understanding of the Seventh Step, in a 1964 issue of the *AA Grapevine*:

> Sins get entangled deep within us, as some roots of a tree, and do not easily come loose. We need help, grace, the lift of a kind of divine derrick (Shoemaker, "Those Twelve Steps as I Understand Them"; *Volume II, Best of the Grapevine*, p. 130).

4. **Taking your own inventory**. James 4:11-12 state:

> Speak not evil one of another, brethren. He that speaketh evil of *his* brother, and judgeth his brother, speaketh evil of the law, and judgeth the law: but if thou judge the law, thou art not a doer of the law, but a judge.
> There is one lawgiver, who is able to save and to destroy: who art thou that judgest another?

We discussed the Fourth Step idea of taking your own inventory in connection with the relevant verses in the Sermon on the Mount–which were often quoted by Oxford Group people and by Anne Smith (See Matt. 7:1-5). But the Big Book also speaks of: (1) looking "for our own mistakes," (2) asking "Where were we to blame," and (3) realizing, "The inventory was ours, not the other man's." Considering the importance to AAs of the Book of James and its insights, the foregoing James verses probably also had an impact on the A.A. idea of avoiding judgment of another and focusing on an examination of one's *own* conduct when it comes to wrongdoing.

**James Chapter 5**

1. **Patience**. We discussed A.A.'s "patience principle" as having probably derived from James, Chapter One. As we said, however, important stress on patience can be found in James 5:7, 8, 10, 11.

2. **Grudges** (covered in A.A.'s 4th Step resentment inventory process). James 5:9 reads:

> Grudge not one against another, brethren, lest ye be condemned; behold, the judge standeth before the door.

A major portion of the Big Book's Fourth Step discussion is devoted to resentment, about which page 64 says:

> Resentment is the "number one" offender. It destroys more alcoholics than anything else. From it stem all forms of spiritual disease.

The Big Book then suggests putting resentments *on paper*—making a *"grudge list"* (pp. 64-65). Oxford Group spokesman Ebenezer Macmillan wrote at length in his title *Seeking and Finding* about eliminating resentments, hatred, or the *"grudge"* that "blocks God out effectively." Rev. Sam Shoemaker also specified "grudges" as one of the "sins" to be examined in an inventory of self (Shoemaker, *Twice-Born Ministers*, p. 182). Since the Big Book lists resentments or
"grudges" as one of the four major "character defects" which block us from God, it quite possible that the "grudge" language in the Big Book was influenced by James, and perhaps specifically by James 5:9.

3. **Asking God's forgiveness for sins**. We repeat James 5:15, which was partially quoted above. The entire verse says:

> And the prayer of faith shall save the sick, and the Lord shall raise him up; and if he have committed sins, they shall be forgiven him.

The Big Book says this about asking God's forgiveness when we fall short:

> If we are sorry for what we have done, and have the honest desire to let God take us to better things, we believe we will be forgiven and will have learned our lesson (4th ed, p. 70).

> When we retire at night, we constructively review our day. . . . After making our review, we ask God's forgiveness and inquire what corrective measures should be taken (4th ed., p. 86).

The foregoing Big Book quotes show that, even after their initial surrender, wrongdoers may still, in A.A.'s view, seek and receive God's forgiveness for shortcomings indulged after the initial surrender. Here again, James has no corner on the statement that God makes it possible, through forgiveness, for a believer to regain fellowship with Him. The following in 1 John 1:9 may also have been a source of such Big Book ideas:

> If we confess our sins, he is faithful and just to forgive us *our* sins, and to cleanse us from all unrighteousness.

See also our discussion of forgiveness in connection with the Sermon on the Mount. It is fair to say, however, that the Book of James, 1 John, or Matthew could each, or all, have been the basis for the Big Book forgiveness concept.

4. **Confess your sins one to another**. It has often been noted that *both* the Oxford Group concept of sharing by confession *and* Step Five in the Big Book were derived from James 5:16:

> Confess your faults one to another, and pray for one another, that ye may be healed.

Of much more significance than "sharing by confession" and the source of Step Five is the direct patterning of Akron's "real surrenders" on this verse and those surrounding it. Akron brothers prayed for the new man. They brought him to Christ. They had him accept Christ and utter his own prayer to be cured and to live by the principles of Christ. The objective was to have him become a Christian, to rely on the power of god, to be cured, and to live by Christian principles.

5. **Effectual, fervent prayer works**. James 5:16 states:

> The effectual fervent prayer of a righteous man availeth much.

A.A.'s Big Book Fourth Edition says:

> Step Eleven suggests prayer and meditation. We shouldn't be shy on this matter of prayer. Better men than we are using it constantly. It works, if we have the proper attitude and work at it.

James 5:16 could well have been a major basis for the Big Book comments on the effectiveness of prayer.

6. **Anointing with oil and effecting healing through prayer by elders. See James 5:13-16.**

One A.A. writer, who was sponsored by Clarence Snyder, has repeatedly suggested that in their "surrenders," early AAs almost literally followed the foregoing verses from James. Others, who also were sponsored by Clarence Snyder, have said this contention is in error. But several comments should be made about this procedure. First, there seems little confirmation that Dr. Bob, T. Henry Williams, and the Akron pioneers took the newcomer "upstairs," had him "surrender" to Christ, anointed him with oil, and prayed for him. Second, many of the elements of the James verses were followed. Third, in his later years, Clarence Snyder founded and conducted retreats for AAs and their families which are still being held. At these retreats, there is a "prayer and praise" session where there is anointing with oil and prayer for those in need. The sessions follow the close of the retreat itself. Finally, we make particular mention of these points because so many of the healing practices of the Christian church throughout later centuries did rely on the words of St. James and did heal with the laying on of hands and anointing with oil. These points are amply covered by the citations in our healing section. They are important because the convictions about "healing" and "cure" were so evident and strong in early A.A.; and the return of healing emphasis–whatever the technique or Biblical authority–is urgently needed in today's Twelve Step programs.

## A Study of 1 Corinthians 13 in A.A.

1 Corinthians 13 is often called the Bible's "love" chapter because it focuses on the importance of love in the Christian's life. In the King James Version, the word "charity" is used in the verses which are speaking of "love;" but the underlying Greek word is *agapē* which is more properly translated "love."

And the most frequently quoted characteristics of love are contained in the following verses from the King James Version of the Bible (which is the version the A.A. pioneers used):

> Charity [love] suffereth long, *and* is kind; charity envieth not; charity vaunteth not itself, is not puffed up,
> Doth not behave itself unseemly, seeketh not her own, is not easily provoked, thinketh no evil;
> Rejoiceth not in iniquity, but rejoiceth in the truth (1 Cor. 13:4-6).

The New International Version, which is much in use today, renders 1 Cor. 13:4-6:

> Love is patient, love is kind. It does not envy, it does not boast, it is not proud.
> It is not rude, it is not self-seeking, it is not easily angered, it keeps no record of wrongs.
> Love does not delight in evil but rejoices with the truth.

One of the most popular books in early A.A. was Professor Henry Drummond's study of 1 Corinthians 13. The title of his book, *The Greatest Thing in the World,* was taken from the last verse of 1 Corinthians chapter 13, which reads:

> And now abideth faith, hope, charity, these three; but the greatest of these is charity (1 Cor. 13:13).

Drummond's book was part of Dr. Bob's library, and a copy was still found in, and owned by, Dr. Bob's family when the author interviewed Dr. Bob's son and daughter several years ago. In much earlier years, A.A. Old-timer Bob E. had sent a memo to Bill Wilson's wife, Lois, in which Bob E. listed *The Greatest Thing in the World* as one of three books Dr. Bob regularly provided to alcoholics with whom he worked. In fact, Dr. Bob's enthusiasm for Drummond's book is dramatized by the following remarks by a former wife of A.A. old-timer Clarence S. Clarence's former wife, Dorothy S. M., said:

> Once, when I was working on a woman in Cleveland, I called and asked him [Dr. Bob], "What do I do for somebody who is going into D.T.'s?" He told me to give her the medication, and he said, "When she comes out of it and she decides she wants to be a different woman, get her Drummond's 'The Greatest Thing in the World.' Tell her to read it through every day for 30 days, and she'll be a different woman"(See *DR. BOB and the Good Oldtimers,* p. 310).

Henry Drummond himself had made a similar suggestion half a century earlier, at the close of the lecture in which he delivered his 'greatest thing in the world' address–the address which was later published in Drummond's best-seller. Drummond said:

> Now I have all but finished. How many of you will join me in reading this chapter [1 Corinthians 13] once a week for the next three months? A man did that once and it changed his whole life. Will you do it? It is for the greatest thing in the world. You might begin by reading it every day, especially the verses which describe the perfect character. "Love suffereth long, and is kind; loveth envieth not; love vaunteth not itself." Get these ingredients into your life (See Drummond, *The Greatest Thing in the World.* p. 53).

The important influence on A.A. that came from 1 Corinthians 13 can be seen in Drummond's own simplified description of love's *ingredients*. Drummond listed nine ingredients of "love" as he saw love specifically defined in that portion of that chapter of the Bible (See Drummond, *The Greatest Thing in the World*, pp. 26-27). And we here set out those nine love ingredients with references to correlative Bible verses and correlative A.A. language:

| **Drummond's Explanation** | **Authorized KJV** | **NIV Version** | **A.A. Big Book 4th ed. Examples** |
|---|---|---|---|
| 1. Patience | "Charity suffereth long." | "Love is patient" | pp. 67, 70, 83, 111, 163 |
| 2. Kindness | "*and* is kind." | "love is kind" | pp. 67, 82, 83, 86 |
| 3. Generosity | "charity envieth not." | "It does not envy" | pp. 145, *cf.* 82 |
| 4. Humility | "charity vaunteth not itself "is not puffed up. | "it does not boast, "it is not proud" | pp. 13, 57, 68, 87-88 |

| | | | |
|---|---|---|---|
| 5. Courtesy | "Doth not behave itself unseemly" | "It is not rude" | p. 69 |
| 6. Unselfishness | "seeketh not her own." | "It is not self-seeking" | pp. xxv, 93,127 |
| 7. Good Temper | "is not easily provoked" | "it is not easily angered | pp. 19, 67, 70, 83-84, 125, 118 |
| "thinketh no evil" | "it keeps no record of wrongs" | | pp. 19, 67, 70, 83-84, 118, 125 |
| 9. Sincerity | "Rejoiceth not in iniquity" "but rejoiceth in the truth" | "does not delight in evil "but rejoices with the truth" | pp. xiv, xxvii, 13, 26, 28, 32, 44, pp. 47, 55, 57-58, 63-65, 67, 70, 73, 117, 140, 145 |

Dr. Bob said that A.A.'s Twelve Steps, when simmered down to the last, quite simply resolved themselves into the words "love" and "service" (See *DR. BOB and the Good Oldtimers*, p. 338). He presented God to the oldtimers as a God of love who was interested in their individual lives. (*DR. BOB, supra*, p. 110). Dr. Bob's wife, Anne, frequently quoted love verses in 1 John 4:8; 4:16–"God is love" (*DR. BOB supra*, pp. 116-17). Furthermore both Anne and her husband Dr. Bob studied Toyohiko Kagawa's book, *Love: The Law of Life.* In that book, the author Kagawa devoted an entire chapter to 1 Corinthians 13, not only to the Corinthians chapter, but also to Drummond's analysis of that chapter in Drummond's *The Greatest Thing in the World.* Hence there was much emphasis among the A.A. pioneers on the "spiritual" principle of love as it is defined in the Bible. In fact, the Big Book itself talks repeatedly of that principle of love (Big Book, 4th ed., pp. 83-84, 86, 118, 122, 153).

Love, then--the love of God--was a much cherished principle in early A.A. The AAs needed it, wanted it, studied it, and sought to know it. Despite "higher power" divergences in current A.A. writings and meeting talk, the love of God is still a vital component of A.A. thinking and speech. Even Bill Wilson inserted the phrase "a loving God" in A.A.'s Traditions. And I well remember my good friend Seymour W., a Jew, who tried each morning to comfort his many friends in the fellowship. The telephone on Seymour's "God" line would ring for many about 6:00 A.M. The message to the bedraggled A.A. was "God loves you." And Seymour would hang up. It was a coveted privilege to be on Seymour's "God-loves-you" list. What a way to start the day in early sobriety!

Further illustrating the great store placed on God's love and on the Corinthians love principle by A.A. pioneers is their frequent rendition of Jesus Christ's message in Mark 12:30-31. These Gospel verses deal with what Jesus called the two *great* commandments:

> And thou shalt love the Lord thy God with all thy heart, and with all thy soul, and with all thy mind, and with all thy strength; this is the first commandment. And the second is like, namely this, Thou shalt love thy neighbor as thyself. There is none other commandment greater than these.

The foregoing verses, from the Gospel of Mark in the New Testament, were cited for the standard of "Absolute Love," as it was discussed in AA of Akron's *A Manual for Alcoholics Anonymous* (one of the four pamphlets commissioned by Dr. Bob for use among early AAs). The Old Testament also contained the very same commandments to which Jesus referred, underlining the importance of love of God and of neighbor in all the commandments of the Bible:

> Hear, O Israel: The Lord our God *is* one Lord: And thou shalt love the Lord thy God with all thine heart, and with all thy soul, and with all thy might (Deut. 6:4-5).
>
> Thou shalt not avenge, nor bear any grudge against the children of thy people, but thou shalt love thy neighbor as thyself: I *am* the Lord (Lev. 19:18).

A.A. literature contains no specifics on, or detailing of, the impact of, 1 Corinthians 13 on A.A. But this cherished "essential," as Dr. Bob put it, deserves to be revived, promulgated, and applied today. The particulars can be seen by reading 1 Corinthians 13 itself; by noting the frequent mention of "Love" in the Big Book; by studying the reading and remarks of Dr. Bob and Anne; by remembering Bill Wilson's specific mention of Corinthians; and by the repeated mention of 1 Corinthians 13 in A.A.'s religious sources. The nine love "ingredients," as they were summarized by Henry Drummond, permeate A.A.'s basic text and can fairly be proclaimed to be among those "principles to be practiced" at the level of A.A.'s Twelfth Step. Regrettably, Wilson just plain ignored all the "principles" in his Twelfth Step chapter.

The fundamental principle is, of course, love. The component "ingredients" or "virtues" involved in such love are: patience; tolerance; kindness; humility; honesty; unselfishness; consideration for others; and the avoidance of anger, jealousy, envy, pride, and wrongdoing.
As previously covered, almost every one of these virtues can be found as well in Jesus' sermon on the mount and in the Book of James. The principles are defined in the sermon on the mount in specific terms that elaborate upon what constitutes doing the will of God in the love

category. And, in James, from the standpoint of action and service to God and service to others through reliance upon God.

These were also the very the principles of love and service of which Dr. Bob spoke in his farewell address and defined as the essence of A.A.'s spiritual program of recovery.

# 7

# The Creator and the Cure of Alcoholism: Miracle or Myth?

## What IS the "Alcoholism" of Which the Pioneers Claimed Cure?

What is "alcoholism?" Dr. Bob called it this terrible curse. Wilson called it "this terrible disease." Some say that liquor is but a symptom. Some call it a spiritual malady. Some call it an obsession of the mind coupled with an allergy of the body. Some call it insanity and incorrectly say that it is doing the same thing over and over and expecting the result to be different. I contest that because we usually know exactly what the result will be–no different at all. What is it?

We alcoholics have a pretty good idea of what it is: We drink too much. We get in trouble. We repeat the self-destructive behavior and often continue it to the point of insanity, imprisonment, and death *(Alcoholics Anonymous*, 4th ed., p. 44). We frequently explain the disastrous consequences by denying them, blaming the whole thing on someone or something else, or flipping them off with, "I don't care" or the pious, "I'll never do that again."

Science, medicine, and religion have often beclouded our simple understanding of the problem. Words and phrases such as genetic, behavior disorder, nutritional imbalance, neurological origin, and (of course) sin leave us puzzled or possessed of an alibi. It's in my genes. I just have trouble adjusting. I'm eating the wrong things. It must be something in my brain. My preacher tells me it's sin. Yet most of us will actually admit on occasion that we had just a little too much to drink, got a little tipsy, got arrested without cause, or fell off the wagon. The scientific definitions really don't say much to the drunk lying on the sidewalk in a puddle of his own urine.

Then there are those pseudo medical condemnations: Alcoholics are "medically incurable"–an assertion that still seems to have medical validity. But then the *non-sequitur*: "Alcoholism is incurable." Worse: "Once an alcoholic always an alcoholic." Translated into some solid fear language, that could as well be rendered, "Once a leper always a leper." As to the Bill Wilson condemnation, there is very probably the following root: Bill probably coined the "once an alcoholic always an alcoholic" expression and "no cure" idea from a therapist named Richard R. Peabody. Apparently Peabody had died drunk–a "victim" of his own therapy. That, said Wilson, proved that alcoholism was "uncurable." And the statement is ridiculous. Moreover, it utterly lacks integrity since neither Wilson nor Peabody was a religious leader, a physician, or in possession of any treatment credentials whatever. As to Wilson's deduction, one analyst commented: The fact that several of Peabody's major practitioners–apparently including the founder–were not able to maintain their sobriety, however, does not bode well for other patients. For me, however, the comment would be that these were a bunch of alcoholics who wanted to drink and didn't seek help from God.

Wilson owned a copy of Peabody's book, *The Common Sense of Drinking*. The book contains this inscription: "Dr. Peabody was as far as is known the first authority to state, "once an alcoholic, always an alcoholic," and he proved it by returning to drinking and by dying of alcoholism–proving to us that the condition is uncurable." If the inscription was made in jest, it's sarcastic. If it was made with sincerity, it is, instead, an absurdity. Either way, it bespeaks the condemnation A.A. people have come to accept. Woe. Woe. Woe: Alcoholism can't be cured. I can't be cured. You can't be cured. Nobody can be cured. So let's go to A.A. and live sober "one day at a time."

Let's look at the real situation at the time A.A. was founded. A.A. members definitely acknowledged that alcoholism was *medically* incurable. Their physicians told them so. Most of those same physicians, however, also told them that "real" alcoholics were: (1) 100% hopeless apart from divine help (*Alcoholics Anonymous*, 4th ed., pp. 26-27. (2) Beyond help except by way of a conversion–where Wilson deleted the "God" part of Dr. Carl Jung's advice; Big Book p. 43. (3) were beyond human help and needed Divine Help–the conclusion of a "staff member of a world-renowned hospital;" pp. 52-57). In fact, Bill Wilson's own physician told a patient (not then in A.A.) that he (Dr. William D. Silkworth–a specialist in treating alcoholism) could not help him, but that the Great Physician, Jesus Christ, could do so!

Richard Peabody's *The Common Sense of Drinking* was written in 1931. Copies were owned and read by both A.A. founders Smith and Wilson. Its language is so similar to that in certain portions of the Big Book that it very possibly caused much of the later A.A. fellowship "incurable alcoholism" legend. Even worse, it may well have been responsible for fallacious ideas characterizing the "problem" as "powerlessness;" the "process" as being "in recovery;" "willpower;"as being useless, and the "solution" as some sort of "surrender" that amounted to a "cure." Wilson seemed to insert or modify those Peabody legacies in the Big Book, Peabody having said the following:

> This man, after thirty-six years of living and approximately sixteen of drinking, has definitely proved to his own conviction that he cannot use alcohol without abusing it, and that by his own efforts he is equally *powerless* to stop his indulgence (p. 37).
>
> He can never again drink anything containing alcohol without the ultimate results being disastrous (p. 96).
>
> Halfway measures are of no avail (p. 99).
>
> He must have as his goal. . . the complete renunciation of the use of alcohol as a beverage in any quantity, however small, for all time (p. 81).
>
> . . . [R]econstruct his mental processes so that in due time he will no longer want to drink. That is what I mean by the necessary "surrender" (p. 80).
>
> Suffice it to say, once a drunkard always a drunkard–or a teetotaler! A fairly exhaustive inquiry has elicited no exceptions to this rule (p. 82).
> Surrendering–that is, being cured. . . (p. 77).
>
> An alcoholic should always realize that he himself does the actual work which produces the cure. . . . We give them the

> desire to be cured, but it is they themselves who work the cure (p. 99).

Those familiar with A.A.'s Big Book will see in a flash how much of the Peabody stuff was codified in Wilson's writing. The difficulty is that the material lacks integrity and credibility. It perpetrates lots of negativity, fear, and ineffective self-help. Surrender became self-surrender. Cure became surrender. Adjustment of one's thinking was substituted for reliance on the power of God. In fact, there was no mention of God. And yet the Peabody stuff became tangled in with the God stuff. But Peabody's stuff lacked the religious element that was the heart of the early solution: (1) Man can't. (2) Humans can't. (3) God can and will and does. Not so with Peabody; and eventually A.A.itself allowed the following revisionism that chimed in with Wilson, embraced the tune, and denied the cure:

> It might also be noted that many terms now considered by A.A. to be misleading were then used, not only by non-A.A.'s discussing the movement, but sometimes by members themselves: "cure," "ex-alcoholic," "reformed alcoholic" [See *DR. BOB and the Good Oldtimers*, *supra*, p. 136].

More's the pity. Define alcoholism as incurable and you make every pioneer from Bill Wilson to Dr. Bob to Bill Dotson and a host of others outright liars. They all said they were cured. And either they were cured, as they said; or they were not. For an excellent discussion of the countless times cure was sought, obtained, claimed, and verified, see Richard K., *Early A.A.--Separating Fact from Fiction: How Revisionists Have Led Our History Astray* (Haverhill, MA: Golden Text Publishing Company, 2003); and Appendix Four of our title.

Peabody was not the only malefactor. In my title *God and Alcoholism: Our Growing Opportunity in the 21st Century* (Kihei, HI: Paradise Research Publications), pp. 24-49, the names and quotes by a sampling of experts are given. The people range from preachers to historians to physicians to psychologists to drunks to authors to religious authorities. They give you any and every kind of definition of alcoholism you might wish to adopt. The definitions range from allergy to sin, with many complexities to boot. The problem is that almost every definition counts

God out! Define something in difficult enough terms, and you rule out the spiritual solution, it seems.

What I do know from the statements of A.A. pioneers, from my own situation, and from working with many new alcoholics is this: If you drink to excess; if you get in trouble; if you are in the wine vat over your head, you can stop the whole thing! You can be cured! How? The same way the pioneers were. You do it the way the pioneers did.

You decide to quit. You decide to do whatever it takes–shivers and shakes along with it. Even the concomitant divorces, bankruptcies, incarcerations, and liver problems. You believe that God is. You believe He can heal you. You stay away from temptation, from trouble, and from booze. You stick with the Creator every step of the way. You decide that God expects some things of you; they're in the Bible; they're well-known to most of us; and they are often called "commandments"–not just Ten. A whole bunch. They are not grievous says the Bible. They are mandatory. So you decide to obey, to confess when you stumble, and to ask God's forgiveness. Then you get up and go with God again. When you see that it works, you start chasing other drunks and telling them your success in exchange for their tales of woe. You give them the same opportunity to be cured. You pray for and with them. Then it's their turn–to pass or fail!

They may never know or learn what "alcoholism" is. But they can sure find out exactly what the peace of God is. They may just be cured!

## The Countless Claims of Cure by Early AAs

I'm going to leave a good deal of documentation of the early cures to the fine work by Richard K's *Early A.A. - Separating Fact From Fiction, supra,*. and, in part, to Appendices 3 and 4 of this title. The broader picture is available in my title *Cured: Proven Help for Alcoholics and Addicts* (Kihei, HI: Paradise Research Publications, 2003).

The objective here is to name for you a few of the hundreds of places where early A.A. members said they were cured, that they'd found a cure, or that others had been cured.

- Bill Wilson - Big Book, 4th ed., p. 191

- Dr. Bob - Big Book, 4th ed., pp. 180, 188
- Bill Dotson (AA Number Three) - Big Book, 4th ed., p. 191
- Clarence Snyder (one of the later, 40 pioneers) - Big Book, 3rd ed., pp. 216-217; Mitchell K., *How It Worked*, pp. 138-139
- Larry Jewell (who was sponsored by Dr. Bob and Clarence and wrote the series of articles in the *Houston Press* in 1940
- Theodore English (who wrote the article in *Scribner's Commentator* in January, 1941)
- Dr. William D. Silkworth (who wrote the Dr.'s Opinion in the Big Book); Norman Vincent Peale, *The Positive Power of Jesus Christ*, pp. 59-63
- Rev. Dilworth Lupton (the Unitarian Minister who wrote the famous "Mister X"); Mitchell K., *How It Worked*, pp. 156, 157.
- The alcoholic who drafted a proposed cover for the Big *Book–The Pathway to a Cure*
- Elrick Davis (who wrote the series of articles in the *Cleveland Plain Dealer*) before his articles were altered by A.A. reprints
- Morris Markey (who wrote the 1939 Liberty Magazine article "Alcoholics and God")
- Paul de Kruif (who wrote the article in A.A.'s own publication); *Volume II, Best of the Grapevine*, pp. 202-203

Author and historian Richard K. has assembled hundreds of references by early A.A. people, by writers about A.A., and by commentators who reported on A.A.'s work. In newspaper article after newspaper article, there appeared such items as:

> "Rockefeller Helps to Cure Alcoholics" (*The Denver Post*)
>
> "Alcoholics Anonymous" An Unusual Liquor Cure (*King Features Syndicate*)

"800 Former Drunkards Pay Tribute to Founders of Cure in Cleveland" (*Akron Beacon*)

"Alcoholics Anonymous Help Drunks Cure Selves, Then Others" (*NY World Telegram*)

"So You Think Drunks Can't Be Cured" (*The Courier-Journal*, Kentucky)

"Cured by their own 'Horrible Examples'" (*The Denver Post*)

"Group of Reformed Alcoholics Cured Him of Habit That Jeopardized Job, Hemsley Says" (*The Cleveland Plain Dealer*)

"Hemsley Tells How He Defeated Liquor: 'I read the Bible some every day and spend a short time in the morning in meditation'" (*Herald Express*, Los Angeles)

"Alcoholics Anonymous Article Stirs Inquiries: Some weeks ago this column published an account of a new cure for alcoholism" (*The Calgary Herald*)

"The basic point about Alcoholics Anonymous is that it is a fellowship of 'cured' alcoholics. And that both old-line medicine and modern psychiatry had agreed on the one point that no alcoholic could be cured. Repeat the astounding fact: These are cured. They have cured each other. They have done it by adopting with each other's aid, what they call 'a spiritual way of life.'" (*The Cleveland Plain Dealer*)

"A Cure for a Curse" (*The Arkansas Gazette*).

There were dozens and dozens of such articles. But who flipped the switch? Who decided the foregoing people were dishonest, misinformed, or wrong? Who "proved" there was no cure? Who proclaimed the doctrine that Almighty God is "powerless" over alcoholism, cannot cure it, and cannot perform miracles as to alcoholics–miracles we all have observed, whether we experienced them ourselves as I have, or simply observed them as countless A.A. people and so many others have?

## There Is Nothing New When It Comes to God's Miracles and Cures

Appendix Three provides detailed outlines of the cures effected by the power of the Creator from the earliest Bible days to the present time. You should check them out. The records are not some drivel from ignorant bystanders. They are truthful accounts from the Bible, from the church, from individual healers, and from observers throughout the ages. Hundreds of thousands of sick people healed by the power of God. Detailed accounts of the people, their maladies, and the healing work. Quite specifically, Yahweh our God, the Creator, has cured, can cure, does cure, and will cure alcoholism. In fact, A.A.'s Big Book Editions–all of them–have flatly declared: "But there is One Who has all power–that One is God. May you find Him now!" *Alcoholics Anonymous*, 4th ed., p. 59. That's what A.A. people believed and reported!

We hear that statement read at almost every A.A. meeting where the Big Book is used. I believed the statement. I counted on it. I still do.

**The Detour**

The clear cut path to God and to cure that was laid out in early A.A. encountered a blockade and consequent detour. This curious change occurred outside the Big Book. Apparently, a tiny few in New York disputed the use of the word "God." Lois Wilson said of the situation: "There was too much God" (*Lois Remembers*, p. 112). "Finally [claimed Lois] it was agreed that the book should present a universal spiritual program, not a religious one, since all drunks were not Christian" (*Lois Remembers*, p. 112).

There's a hot one for you. In Akron, they were cured by God. Bill Wilson said he was cured by God. Lois Wilson said that God had done for Bill what she could not do. Nonetheless, Lois Wilson–the non-Christian, who didn't think she needed conversion and didn't like the Oxford Group–claimed, without proof, that there was some alleged (but apparently non-existent) A.A. "agreement" to delete God. She did not say there was no God. She did not say that God was not-god. She did not say that alcoholics were not-god. She simply said there was "too much" God.

How you get "too much God" is a puzzler for me. But apparently not for Lois's husband. Bill responded. He took "God" out of the Second Step language. He utilized the Oxford Group "as we understood Him" idea in the Third and Eleventh Steps. Yet he left "God" in, over 400 times. Not much of a victory for Lois, but a sad day indeed for Alcoholics Anonymous.

Bill invented a "powerless" to "power" theology in his step progression. It was just plain self-made religion. The process spawned absurd names for God, and it resulted in half-baked prayers that Shoemaker himself had criticized from his very first book forward.

Having proclaimed alcoholics were "powerless," Bill decided there was need to find a "power." And–though the "Power" in the Oxford Group was Almighty God–the A.A. "Power" became one to be defined in all sorts of ridiculous terms, by humans, not by God. This in turn invited atheists, agnostics, skeptics, and critics to assume the "power" was a "limited power." If anything, it was merely a "power" that could "remove" the obsession, but was "powerless" to cure the allergy. What a strange power that lacks power! This faulty reasoning opened the door to claiming that "relapses" must be due to activation of the allergy, rather than due to failure and temptation. Wide open, then, was the door to Bill's championing of missions, hospitals, treatment, and therapy.

Where was God? Since the "power" could be any old power, any old god, any old something, universalism was just around the corner–agreed to or not. And what an invitation for book sales, large royalties, ever growing membership turnover–and ineffective results. Lots of room for more. A "theology" that: (1) accepts agnostics, atheists, and unbelievers; (2) accepts the idea that the "power" and "limited cure" will be available to anyone anywhere at any price. But the problem is that there is no power on earth that can stop an alcoholic from drinking if he or she wants to. Moreover, there is no cure on earth that has been evolved in a laboratory, a seminary, or a medical school. The situation, however, does not prove that the power of God cannot bring about a cure.

Early A.A. found and depended upon the solution–one that worked. Their views differed markedly from those embracing today's universalism, powerlessness, and Godlessness. It is fair to say that the pioneers believed this: We are *not* powerless over alcohol. We *do* encounter a "power shortage." You might call it a "willpower shortage." It's a shortage that means willpower will yield to temptation. That yielding, that failure to resist, that heeding of devilish ideas is the location of the power shortage. James 4:7 said submit yourselves to God; it then said resist. And the answer is "power"–not "lack of power." It's the power of Almighty God, Yahweh our Creator. All the power we need is available through the Creator, our God, they believed. Dr. Bob said the Creator will never let you down.

The *pioneers* had no problem admitting they were "licked." They were licked. However, in studying James (their favorite book in the Bible), they could conclude that they were licked primarily through giving in to temptation. They didn't lack will power. They could will themselves into a bar and a bottle anytime they wanted to. They lacked sane thinking. Sane reasoning that would give them the ability to resist temptation. They thought, despite their repeated disasters, that they didn't need to resist drinking. That was sick thinking. They had lacked resort to the Creator for sanity, but it was available. "For God hath not given us the spirit of fear; but of power, and of love, and of a sound mind" (2 Timothy 1:7). They simply needed to come to God through Christ, to put the truth of God's Word in their hearts, to believe it, and then march forward in obedience to God, engaging in Godly behavior, and hanging out with like-minded believers. Then they'd know.

Thanks be to God, there was an answer to the insanity that yielded to temptation, to drunkenness, and to their repeated suffering as "real" alcoholics. They could be, were, and had been, transformed by the renewing of their minds (Romans 12:2). They could obey God's commandments against excess (Romans 12:1-2). They could ask for God's guidance and strength in their resistance to alcohol's temptation. This victory was not achieved on their own. It was not merely achieved with the help of other people–whether religious, medical, or drunks. The pioneers rejected the idea that a "human" power provided the cure. What was needed, they said, was to establish a relationship with God, ask Him to take alcohol out of their lives, and diligently try to follow His plan in obedience to His Word. This did not call for the impossible. It called for the miraculous.

**Back on the Path to Yahweh–to Forgiveness, Healing, and Accomplishing the "Impossible"**

Psalm 103:2-3 declares:

> Bless the Lord, O my soul, and forget not all his benefits. Who forgiveth all thine iniquities; who healeth all thy diseases; Who redeemeth thy life from destruction; who crowneth thee with lovingkindness and tender mercies.

Luke 1:35, 37, 38:

> And the angel answered and said unto her, The Holy Ghost shall come upon thee, and the power of the Highest shall overshadow thee: therefore also that holy thing which shall be born of thee shall be called the Son of God.
> For with God nothing shall be impossible.
> And Mary said, Behold the handmaid of the Lord: be it unto me according to thy word. And the angel departed from her.

Let's talk about the original A.A. program that was developed primarily in Akron between 1935 and 1938. Let's talk about what they called "Their pathway to a cure" (See the original cover of this title–which specifically spoke of the pathway to a cure). And let's talk about their path to a relationship with God. And there are several, simple ways of describing it.

One way is thus: Medicine defined their problem. Religion defined their solution. Almighty God enabled the miracle–a healing and a cure. And drunks carried the message to other drunks. Each facet should be given its credit. Of course, one could say the medical definition has been altered or discarded. One could say that religion had less to do with A.A. ideas than the Holy Bible. One could say that the "God-business" somehow gave way to devilish business–the discarding of the definition, the solution, and Divine Aid in favor of endless attendance at meetings.

If you stick to Bill Wilson's attempted description in the Big Book of "Their pathway to a cure," you can still find all the elements of the original program. You can find a "medically incurable" and seemingly hopeless condition of mind and body–and a good deal else. You can find a good many reasons why alcoholics truly had blocked themselves from God–truly were separated from Him, and truly needed to get back into a relationship and fellowship with Him. Such reasoning can be found all through the Big Book. Even today. For Bill Wilson really did really pen his twelve "steps" to a relationship with the Creator. As the whole crowd of pioneer A.A. people saw it, the Big Book paved the way for them by the guidance of the Good Book.

Let's look again. The pathway required recognition of the problem. The problem was excessive drinking. It was boozing out of control. The problem was: "I can't." The pathway required recognition of human limitations. Nobody they knew or met had come up with a treatment plan, a therapeutic process, or a confinement that would assure recovery and cure. This meant: "They can't." The pathway absolutely required that they seek Divine Aid, seek the power and guidance of the Creator, and rely on Him. This meant: "God can."

The key in the Bible can be found in a verse very popular with the pioneers and frequently quoted by Sam Shoemaker and other Oxford Group writers:

> But without faith it is impossible to please him: for he that cometh to God must believe that he is, and that he is a rewarder of them that diligently seek him (Hebrews 11:6).

God either is, or He isn't. Shoemaker wrote that. Wilson put it in the big Book. He added: God could and would if He were sought.

## Cure! A Miracle or a Myth? You Decide

Two of my latest titles are devoted to the subjects of *God and Alcoholism* and *Cured*. (See http://www.dickb.com/titles.shtml). If you want to know whether alcoholism is curable or not, you need to start with an open Bible in front of you. If you can't accept what that Word of God says, you might as well give your Bible to someone who can.

Do you believe in God? That's what Dr. Bob wanted to know and on a "take it or leave it basis." Do you believe that God is? Bill Wilson and his spiritual mentor Sam Shoemaker suggested you had better take a risk–either God is or He isn't. Do you want to suffer, or do you want to seek God and what He has to offer you. Do you believe: "Once an alcoholic, always an alcoholic?" If you do, you might as well stand on a street corner and yell, "Once a leper, always a leper." You couldn't have told that to Jesus because he healed lepers. Do you think you could have told Jesus he couldn't possibly heal an alcoholic? If you do, you might as well forget the verses that say, "With God, nothing is impossible" and that you can do what Jesus did because he went to His father and sent the gift of the Holy Spirit to those who believed.

Let's not beat these points to death. But let's repeat them one more time. Genesis 1:1 says that God created the heavens and the earth. That's all the power we know of. The Book of James tells you that God doesn't tempt you and can't be tempted. The problem lies when you listen to the evil whispers, consider the enticements, and jump back in the puddle without once turning to God. God created the heavens and the earth. God is. God is Yahweh, not some muddle-headed "something." Yahweh loves, heals, cares, and delivers.

Next time you are thinking of drinking, turn first to God. Do what the early A.A. pioneers did when they were cured. Ask Yahweh, in the name of Jesus Christ, to help you kick the temptation out the back door. Believe God has given you the sanity, the power, and the love to be delivered, to be safe, and to resist the Devil. Believe it, walk out on that belief, and see. It's no myth. If it were, then hundreds, if not millions of people, were merely living in an illusion when God healed them, forgave them and delivered them from the power of darkness because they had become His kids and needed His help.

Believe and receive. It's no myth. If it had been a myth, A.A. would never have been born! If it had been a myth, the founders and early A.A. people would never have kept repeating the statement that they had been "cured." If it had been a myth, the hundreds of newspaper articles would never have been written. We should never have acceded to the myth that once you are an alcoholic, you are always an alcoholic. The slogan should have been and can be: "Once an alcoholic............Cured by the power of the Creator." That's for me. I'm one of God's kids; so were those pioneers, and He's with me all the time–whether I ask for His help or not.

END

# Appendix 1

## The Creator's Personal Name Is Yahweh!

We will now go into considerable detail about the name of the Creator of the heavens and the earth, **Yahweh**. Please review this material carefully, as it will answer many questions you may have had about the God Who is the Creator.

### The Creator's Personal Name Is Yahweh

In the main body of this work, we stated that the personal name of the Creator of the heavens and the earth is the Hebrew word *YHWH*, which most modern biblical scholars believe is best represented in English as "Yahweh." For example:

> Yahweh, the proper name of the God of Israel [Francis Brown, with the Cooperation of S. R. Driver and Charles A. Briggs, *The New Brown-Driver-Briggs-Gesenius Hebrew and English Lexicon* (n.p.: Christian Copyrights, 1983), "YHWH" (spelled in Hebrew letters), p. 217 ("BDB")]

> The Reader will immediately notice that the personal name of the biblical God appears in this volume as "YHWH" [Everett Fox, The Five Books of Moses (New York: Schocken Books, 1995), p. xxix]

> The personal name of God is Yahweh. It is a foreign name, quite un-English, and so unlike the good Anglo-Saxon word 'God'. For that reason, if perhaps for no other, the name Yahweh must be preserved. . . . [David J. A. Clines, "Yahweh and the God of Christian Theology," *Theology* 83 (1980), pp. 323-30)]

**The Creator's Name Is Not "God"**

Perhaps you are like many people who have been taught or believe that "God" is God's name, so to speak. The word "God"—as used in the KJV (and in the NIV) in reference to the Creator of the heavens and the earth—is really a title. This can be seen clearly from verses such as the following:

> And I will make thee swear by the LORD [Yahweh], the God **of heaven**, and the God **of the earth**, that thou shalt not take a wife unto my son of the daughters of the Canaanites, among whom I dwell: (Gen 24:3; emphasis added)
> And the LORD [Yahweh] appeared unto him the same night, and said, I *am* the God **of Abraham thy father**: fear not, for I *am* with thee, and will bless thee, and multiply thy seed for my servant Abraham's sake. (Gen 26:24; emphasis added)
>
> And I will take you to me for **a people**, and I will be to you **a God**: and ye shall know that *I am* the LORD [Yahweh] **your God**, which bringeth you out from under the burdens of the Egyptians. (Exod 6:7; emphasis added)
>
> And I will dwell among the children of Israel, and will be **their God**.
> And they shall know that I am the LORD [Yahweh] **their God**, that brought them forth out of the land of Egypt, that I may dwell among them: I am the LORD [Yahweh] **their God**. (Exod 29:45, 46; emphasis added)

The Hebrew word translated "God" in Genesis 1:1 and in the verses immediately above is *elohim*, Strong's number 430 (pronounced "el-o-heem"). This plural Hebrew noun occurs a total of 2,606 times in the Hebrew Old Testament text from which the KJV was translated [BLB, ( www.blueletterbible.org)], and 2,600 times in that from which the NIV was translated (HECOT, p. 98). *Elohim* is translated as the singular English word "God"—as a plural of majesty or a plural intensive with a singular meaning—more than 2,300 times in both the KJV and the NIV, beginning with Genesis 1:1. And it is by far the word most commonly translated "God" in the Old Testament.

The *New Bible Dictionary* explains the Hebrew word *elohim* as follows:

> Though a plural form (*elohim*), Elohim can be treated as a singular, in which case it means the one supreme deity, and in [English versions] is rendered "God." Like its English equivalent, it is, grammatically considered, a common noun, and conveys the notion of all that belongs to the concept of deity, in contrast with man (Nu. 23:19) and other created beings. It is appropriate to cosmic and world-wide relationships (Gn. 1:1), because there is only one supreme and true God, . . . [I]t approaches the character of a proper noun, while not losing its abstract and conceptual quality. . . .
> Strictly speaking, Yahweh is the only "name" of God (*New Bible Dictionary*, 2d ed., organizing ed., J. D. Douglas., under "God, Names of," pp. 429-30.)

And Barker states in *The NIV: The Making of a Contemporary Translation*:

> God himself identifies his name as Yahweh in Exodus 3:15; 6:3. Strictly speaking, all other "names" are either generic terms (e.g., *Elohim*, "God") or apellative [sic] titles or epithets (e.g., *Adonai*, "Lord") [Barker, "YHWH Sabaoth: 'The Lord Almighty'" (http://www.gospelcom.net/ibs/niv/mct/9.php)]

(For more information on the occurrences and meaning of the Hebrew word *elohim*, see *BDB*, p. 43.)

**The Creator's Name Is Not "the LORD"**

Since the Creator's name is actually Yahweh, why did the KJV and many modern versions (such as the NIV and the NASV) translate *YHWH* as "(the) LORD" in Isa. 42:8 and nearly all other places?

> I am **the LORD** [Yahweh]: that is my name: and my glory will I not give to another, neither my praise to graven images (Isa. 42:8 KJV).

> I am **the LORD** [Yahweh]; that is my name! I will not give my glory to another or my praise to idols (Isa. 42:8 NIV).

To understand how the more familiar terms "[the] LORD" and "Jehovah" came to be substituted for the Creator's name, Yahweh, we begin with the discussion of "Yahweh" in the Preface to the NIV:

> In regard to the divine name *YHWH*, commonly referred to as the *Tetragrammaton*, the translators adopted the device used in most English versions of rendering that name as "LORD" in capital letters to distinguish it from *Adonai*, another Hebrew word rendered "Lord," for which small letters are used. Whenever the two names stand together in the Old Testament as a compound name of God, they are rendered "Sovereign LORD." (quoted in the *Interlinear NIV Hebrew-English Old Testament*, p. xxxv).

The Hebrew word *adonai*—Strong's number 136 (pronounced "ad-o-noy'")—means "lord" (BDB, pp. 10, 11). It occurs 442 times in the Hebrew Old Testament underlying the NIV (HECOT, p. 29); and the NIV always translates it as some form of "lord" (i.e., "the Lord," "Lord," and "the Lord's"), except where it is translated "Sovereign," as explained in the NIV Preface quoted above. *Adonai* is translated as some form of "lord" in 433 of the 434 places where it occurs in the Hebrew Old Testament underlying the KJV. (It is translated "God" once in the KJV.)

You may have already anticipated the problem which the NIV, and other modern translations—including the NASV and the Revised Standard Version (RSV)—caused for themselves by choosing not to translate *YHWH* as the proper name "Yahweh." When *YHWH* is used with *adonai*, the NIV (and other translations which took its tack) had to change the translation (and meaning) of *adonai* to "Sovereign" (or something else) in order to avoid an awkward translation like "Lord LORD." We can see this clearly in the first two occurrences of *adonai* in the Hebrew Old Testament (where, in both cases, it is used together with *YHWH*).

> But Abram said, "O Sovereign LORD [*adonai YHWH*], what can you give me since I remain childless and the one who will inherit my estate is Eliezer of Damascus?"
> But Abram said, "O Sovereign LORD [*adonai YHWH*], how can I know that I will gain possession of it?" (Gen. 15:2, 8 NIV)

To see the appropriate solution to this "dilemma" (which the NIV and other translations caused for themselves), we now turn to the Introduction of the *Interlinear NIV Hebrew-English Old Testament* [previously published as *The NIV Interlinear Hebrew-English Old Testament* (NIVIHEOT)]:

> The proper name of God . . . [*YHWH*] is translated "LORD" in the NIV and most other English versions. The NIVIHEOT consistently renders this name as "Yahweh." This is the spelling and pronunciation generally acknowledged by Bible scholars. Further, according to Scripture, this is God's special name, and it has no direct connection with the idea of lordship. Thus the use of the name Yahweh is a major—and, I think, meaningful—exception to the NIV. (pp. xx, xxi).

The JB translation illustrates how the use of God's name, Yahweh, in the English translation accurately and clearly sets forth the truth.

> 'My Lord Yahweh,' Abram replied 'what do you intend to give me? I go childless...'
> 'My Lord Yahweh,' Abram replied 'how am I to know that I shall inherit it?' (Gen. 15:2, 8 JB)

Here is how the KJV translates *adonai* in these two verses:

> And Abram said, Lord GOD [*adonai YHWH*] , what wilt thou give me, seeing I go childless, and the steward of my house [is] this Eliezer of Damascus?
> And he said, Lord GOD [*adonai YHWH*], whereby shall I know that I shall inherit it? (Gen. 15:2, 8 KJV)

The KJV uses the "device" here of translating *YHWH* as "GOD" in small capitals when it follows *adonai* ("lord") in the Hebrew Old Testament. This is certainly no better than the NIV's "device," as *YHWH* also does not mean "God," the English word normally used to translate the Hebrew word *elohim* in the Old Testament.

God's name is not "the LORD." It is Yahweh!

**The Creator's Name Is Not "Jehovah"**

Before "Yahweh" became commonly accepted among modern biblical scholars as the best representation in English of the Hebrew word YHWH, several older translations and versions chose to translate it as "Jehovah." Included in this group were the Darby Translation (DT, 1890), the Young's Literal Translation of the Bible (YLT, 1898), and the American Standard Version (ASV, 1901). These versions have recently become readily accessible through the Internet at sites such as "The Bible Gateway" (http://bible.gospelcom.net/) and the "Blue Letter Bible"

(BLB), (http://www.blueletterbible.org/)]. We again look at Isa. 42:8:

> I am Jehovah, that is my name; and my glory will I not give to another, neither my praise to graven images (DT).
>
> I [am] Jehovah, this [is] My name, And Mine honour to another I give not, Nor My praise to graven images (YLT).
>
> I am Jehovah, that is my name; and my glory will I not give to another, neither my praise unto graven images (ASV).

The Internet version of the *Encyclopaedia Britannica* (http://www.britannica.com/), in its article on "Yahweh," explains how the word "Jehovah" came into being as a translation of *YHWH*:

> Yahweh
>
> the God of the Israelites, his name being revealed to Moses as four Hebrew consonants (YHWH) called the tetragrammaton. After the Exile (6th century BC), and especially from the 3rd century BC on, Jews ceased to use the name Yahweh for two reasons. As Judaism became a universal religion through its proselytizing in the Greco-Roman world, the more common noun Elohim, meaning "god," tended to replace Yahweh to demonstrate the universal sovereignty of Israel's God over all others. At the same time, the divine name was increasingly regarded as too sacred to be uttered; it was thus replaced vocally in the synagogue ritual by the Hebrew word Adonai ("My Lord"), which was translated as Kyrios ("Lord") in the Septuagint, the Greek version of the Old Testament.
>
> The Masoretes, who from about the 6th to the 10th century worked to reproduce the original text of the Hebrew Bible, replaced the vowels of the name YHWH with the vowel signs of the Hebrew words Adonai or Elohim. Thus, the artificial name Jehovah (YeHoWaH) came into being. Although Christian scholars after the Renaissance and Reformation periods used the term Jehovah for YHWH, in the 19th and 20th centuries biblical scholars again began to use the form Yahweh.

The KJV translated *YHWH* as "LORD" with small capitals in more than 6,500 of its 6,824 occurrences in the Hebrew Old Testament [BLB (http://www.blueletterbible.org/)]. In many of the remaining occurrences, *YHWH* was translated "GOD" when it immediately followed *adonai* in the Hebrew text. However, in four other instances—Exod. 6:3; Ps. 83:18; Isa. 12:2; and Isa. 26:4—the KJV translated *YHWH*, Yahweh, as "Jehovah." And *YHWH*, used in conjunction with another Hebrew word, is translated as a compound name including "Jehovah" three times in the KJV: Gen. 22:14; Exod. 17:15; and Jud. 6:24. We will now briefly examine each of the seven places where *YHWH*, Yahweh, is translated as a form of "Jehovah" in the KJV.

The first of the four places where "Jehovah" stands by itself in the KJV is in Book of Exodus.

> And God [*elohim*] spake unto Moses, and said unto him, I am the LORD [*YHWH*, Yahweh]:
> And I appeared unto Abraham, unto Isaac, and unto Jacob, by *the name of* God Almighty [*el shaddai*], but by my name JEHOVAH [*YHWH*, Yahweh] was I not known to them (Exod. 6:2, 3; English words italicized in the original)

In verse two, the KJV translated *YHWH* as "the LORD" according to its normal pattern. However, in verse three, where God (*elohim*) specifically speaks of "my name," *YHWH* is translated as "Jehovah." The words "the name of" in the first part of verse three are in italics in the KJV to indicate that there were no corresponding Hebrew words in the Hebrew Old Testament text underlying the KJV. Thus Exod. 6:3 is not saying that "God Almighty"—*el shaddai* in Hebrew—is a name of God. It is saying that God's name is *YHWH*, Yahweh.

The second occurrence of "Jehovah" standing by itself in the KJV occurs in the Book of Psalms.

> That *men* may know that thou, whose name alone *is* JEHOVAH [*YHWH*, Yahweh], *art* the most high over all the earth (Ps. 83:18)

Here again we see that God's name is *YHWH*, Yahweh.

The last two places where "Jehovah" stands by itself in the KJV are both in the Book of Isaiah.

> Behold, God *is* my salvation; I will trust, and not be afraid: for the LORD JEHOVAH [*YH YHWH*] is my strength and *my* song; he also is become my salvation (Isa. 12:2)

> Trust ye in the LORD [*YHWH*, Yahweh] for ever: for in the LORD JEHOVAH [*YH YHWH*] *is* everlasting strength (Isa. 26:4)

Strangely, in Isa. 26:4 above, *YHWH* is translated as "the LORD" in the first part of the verse and as "Jehovah" in the second part of the verse. *YH* (Yah)—Strong's number 3050—is translated as "the LORD" in Isa. 12:2 and in Isa. 26:4 (the second "the LORD"). It is a shortened form of Yahweh (BDB, p. 219). The two separate words—Yah and Yahweh—are distinguished in the DT as follows:

> . . . for Jah [*YH*, Yah], Jehovah [*YHWH*, Yahweh], is my strength and song, and he is become my salvation (Isa. 12:2b DT)

> . . . for in Jah [*YH*, Yah], Jehovah [*YHWH*, Yahweh], is the rock of ages (Isa. 26:4b DT)

In each of the four verses above, the KJV broke with its normal pattern of translating *YHWH* as "the LORD," but without real justification or explanation.

Genesis chapter 22 contains one of the three places where the KJV translates *YHWH* as "Jehovah," when it occurs in conjunction with another Hebrew word, to form a compound name. (These compound names are sometimes known as the "Jehovah titles." See, for example, The Companion Bible, Appendix 4: "The Divine Names and Titles.")

> And Abraham called the name of that place Jehovahjireh [*YHWH* + *ra'ah*]: as it is said to this day, In the mount of the LORD [*YHWH*, Yahweh] it shall be seen [*ra'ah*] (Gen. 22:14)

The Hebrew verb *ra'ah*, "to see" [Strong's number 7200 (pronounced "raw-ah'")], is simply transliterated in English as "jireh" in the first part of the verse above, and tacked onto the end of "Jehovah" to form "Jehovahjireh." In the second part of the verse, *ra'ah* is translated "it shall be seen." Earlier in the same chapter, *ra'ah* is translated "will provide" in verse 8: ". . . God [*elohim*] will provide [*ra'ah*] himself a lamb for a burnt offering: . . ." The JB reflects this sense of *ra'ah* as "to provide" in its translation of verse 14:

> Abraham called this place 'Yahweh provides', and hence the saying today: On the mountain Yahweh provides.

Once the verb *ra'ah* is translated as a form of "provide" in its three occurrences in verses 8 and 14, one can begin to see the exciting parallel between this record and God's later providing of His Son, Jesus Christ, as a sacrificial offering:

> For God so loved the world, that he gave his only begotten Son, that whosoever believeth in him should not perish, but have everlasting life (John 3:16).

Exodus chapter 17 contains the second place where the KJV translates *YHWH* as "Jehovah," when it occurs in conjunction with another Hebrew word, to form a compound name.

> And Moses built an altar, and called the name of it Jehovahnissi [*YHWH* + *nes*] (Exod. 17:15)

Here, the Hebrew noun *nes* [Strong's number 5251 (pronounced "nace")] is transliterated in English as "nissi" and added onto the end of "Jehovah" to form "Jehovahnissi." Meanings of *nes* include "something lifted up, standard, signal, signal pole, ensign, banner, sign, sail" (Blue Letter Bible). The *Brown-Driver-Briggs Hebrew Lexicon* (BDB) states that *nes* in this verse has the meaning of a "*standard*, as rallying-point, . . . [i.e.,] *my standard*" (emphasis in the original). Thus, the meaning of *YHWH* combined with *nes* in verse 17 above is "Yahweh my banner" or "Yahweh my standard." The Schocken Bible, Volume 1, The Five Books of Moses (SB)—which uses "YHWH" in place of "Yahweh"—translates verse 17 as follows:

> Moshe built a slaughter-site [i.e., altar] and called its name: YHWH My Banner.

Judges chapter 6 contains the final place where the KJV translates *YHWH* as "Jehovah," when it occurs in conjunction with another Hebrew word, to form a compound name.

> And the LORD [*YHWH*, Yahweh] said unto him, Peace [*shalom*] be unto thee; fear not: thou shalt not die.
> Then Gideon built an altar there unto the LORD [*YHWH*, Yahweh], and called it Jehovahshalom [*YHWH+shalom*]: unto this day it is yet in Ophrah of the Abiezrites (Judges 6:23, 24)

The Hebrew noun *shalom* [Strong's number 7965 (pronounced "shaw-lome'")] is transliterated in English as "shalom" and added onto the end of "Jehovah" to form "Jehovahshalom." Meanings of the *shalom* include "completeness, soundness, welfare, peace" (BDB). *Shalom* is usually translated "peace" in the KJV, and BDB indicates that it has that meaning in verse 24 (pp. 1022-23). Thus, the meaning of *YHWH* combined with *shalom* in verse 24 above is "Yahweh is (or perhaps "gives" or "sends") peace." The JB translates the verse as follows:

> Gideon built an altar there to Yahweh and called it Yahweh-Peace. This altar still stands at Ophrah of Abiezer (Judges 6:24 JB)

Thus we can see that the Creator's name, Yahweh, could easily have been used in the seven unusual places where the KJV translated *YHWH* as "Jehovah."

**What about the So-called "Names of God?"**

After this extended discussion of the Creator's name, Yahweh, you may be wondering: "But I thought God had many names in the Bible." Indeed, such books as *The Names of GOD in Holy Scripture* by Andrew Jukes (Grand Rapids, MI: Kregel, 1967) and *Names of God* by Nathan Stone (Chicago: Moody Press, 1944) would certainly lead one to believe that the Creator of the heavens and the earth had many names. Books with titles such as those just mentioned notwithstanding, scholars almost universally acknowledge that the Creator has only one proper name in Old Testament–*YHWH*, Yahweh:

> Strictly speaking, Yahweh is the only "name" of God. In Genesis wherever the word *sem* ("name") is associated with the divine being that name is Yahweh. When Abraham or Isaac built an altar "he called on the name of Yahweh" (Gn. 12:8; 13:4; 26:25) [*New Bible Dictionary*, under "God, Names of," pp. 429ff.]

> God himself identifies his name as Yahweh in Exodus 3:15; 6:3. Strictly speaking, all other "names" are either generic terms (e.g., *Elohim*, "God") or apellative [sic] titles or epithets (e.g., *Adonai*, "Lord") [Barker, *The NIV*, chapter on "YHWH Sabaoth" (http://www.gospelcom.net/ibs/niv/mct/9.php)]

> Yahweh, the proper name of the God of Israel [Under "YHWH" (spelled in Hebrew letters), BDB, p. 217]

Yahweh is **the** personal, proper name of the Creator of the heavens and the earth!

## The Creator's Name in the New Testament

We have seen that the Creator's name, Yahweh, occurs approximately 6,824 times in the Hebrew Old Testament. But what about in the New Testament? There are four verses in the Book of Revelation that contain a form of the name of Yahweh in the KJV:

> And after these things I heard a great voice of much people in heaven, saying, **Alleluia**; Salvation, and glory, and honour, and power, unto the Lord our God:
> And again they said, **Alleluia** And her smoke rose up for ever and ever.
> And the four and twenty elders and the four beasts fell down and worshipped God that sat on the throne, saying, Amen; **Alleluia**.
> And I heard as it were the voice of a great multitude, and as the voice of many waters, and as the voice of mighty thunderings, saying, **Alleluia**: for the Lord God omnipotent reigneth.(Rev. 19:1, 3, 4, 6; emphasis added)

The English word "Alleluia" in the four verses above [Greek *allelouia* (Strong's number 239)] is translated "Hallelujah" in the NIV, the NASV, and the RSV. Strong's Concordance states that *allelouia* is of Hebrew origin and etymologically derives from the Hebrew verb *halal*, "to praise" [pronounced "haw-lal'" (Strong's number 1984)], and from *Yah* (Strong's number 3050), the shortened form or contraction for Yahweh. In other words, the Greek word *allelouia* means "Praise Yah(weh)." For example, look at the following verse from Ps. 104:

> Let the sinners be consumed out of the earth, and let the wicked be no more. Bless thou the LORD, O my soul. Praise ye [*halal*] the LORD [*YH*, Yah] (Ps. 104:35)

The Interlinear NIV Hebrew-English Old Testament translates the clause "Praise ye the LORD" in verse 35 as "Praise Yahweh."

Another aspect of studying the use of the Creator's name in the New Testament is to look
at verses from the Old Testament that are quoted in the New Testament.

> The LORD [*YHWH*, Yahweh] said unto my Lord [*adon*], "Sit thou at my right hand, until I make thine enemies thy footstool." (Ps. 110:1)

The second "Lord" in the verse above is the translation of the Hebrew word *adon*—Strong's number 113 (pronounced "aw-done'")—and means "lord" or "master," and is usually so translated in the KJV and other English versions such as the NIV.

> And David himself saith in the book of Psalms, The LORD [*kurios*] said unto my Lord [*kurios*], Sit thou on my right hand, Till I make thine enemies thy footstool. (Lu. 20:42, 43)

Even though the KJV put the first "LORD" in small capitals (which in the Old Testament would indicate that it was the Hebrew word *YHWH*, Yahweh), both occurrences of "Lord" in the verse 42 above are translations of the Greek word *kurios*—Strong's number 2962 (pronounced "koo'-ree-os"). According to *Young's Analytical Concordance to the Bible*, *kurios* means "lord, sir, master," and it is usually translated as "lord" in the KJV.

You can probably already see the problem that arises in trying to track the Creator's name through the New Testament. The Hebrew Old Testament consistently uses *YHWH*, Yahweh, for the Creator's name and etymologically unrelated words for "lord" [including *adon* and *adonai* (which comes from *adon*)]. The Greek New Testament, however, uses *kurios*—the Greek equivalent of the Hebrew *adon* and *adonai*—to represent both the Creator's name Yahweh and the Hebrew word for "lord," *adon(ai)*.

The historical and other reasons why the Creator's personal name, Yahweh, does not occur in any publicly known manuscripts of the Greek New Testament are beyond the scope of this present discussion. However, learning as much as you can about the use of the Creator's personal name throughout the Bible will make for a very rewarding study.

# Appendix 2

## Rev. Sam Shoemaker, an A.A. "Co-Founder" and Spiritual Source

### An Introduction to Sam Shoemaker and A.A.

Bill Wilson often said: Reverend Samuel Shoemaker was a wellspring of the principles and attitudes that came to full flower in A.A.'s Twelve Steps for Recovery; that Sam's early teachings did much to inspire him and Dr. Bob; and, that from Shoemaker, he and Dr. Bob in the beginning absorbed most of the Twelve Step principles. Then, at A.A.'s 1955 International Convention, Bill declared that early A.A. got its ideas of self-examination, acknowledgment of character defects, restitution for harm done, and working with others directly from Sam Shoemaker. Later, Bill added that early AAs learned about moral inventory, amends for harm done, turning their wills and lives over to God, meditation and prayer "and all the rest of it" straight from the Oxford Group as it was "then led in America" by Dr. Shoemaker. Finally, Bill wrote to Sam himself in 1963: "The Twelve Steps of A.A. simply represented an attempt to state in more detail, breadth, and depth, what we had been taught–primarily by you." Bill also said:"Without this, there could have been nothing–nothing at all." Bill then added Sam Shoemaker's name to his list of "co-founders" of A.A.

There is much more. Sam was the Episcopal Rector at Calvary Church in New York, the church which operated Calvary Rescue Mission where both Bill Wilson and his "sponsor" Ebby Thacher made their decisions for Christ. Ebby's Oxford Group mentors Rowland Hazard and Shep Cornell were much involved with Sam's Calvary Church at that time. When Bill emerged from Towns Hospital in late 1934, Sam immediately asked Bill to help Professor Frederick E. Breithut with his drinking problem. In March, 1935, Bill, as godfather, sponsored the baptism of Breithut by Sam Shoemaker. Ebby himself became a communicant at Calvary Church. And the relationship of Bill and his early friends with Sam, and with Oxford Group meetings at Calvary House and Oxford Group meetings and houseparties led by Shoemaker was close and continuous. In the mid to late 1930's, Bill spent many hours closeted with Sam in Sam's book-lined study at Calvary House, discussing the spiritual ideas which were soon to characterize A.A.

Even more important are these facts: Bill actually asked Sam Shoemaker to write the Twelve Steps; but Sam declined, saying the Steps should be written by an alcoholic, namely, Bill. Then, when Bill had completed the Big Book manuscript, he circulated it to Sam for review prior to publication. Also, Sam's reach into early A.A. actually extended much farther than New York. For Dr. Bob's pastor in Ohio wrote to Sam advising him of the progress with alcoholics in Akron as a result of Bill's stay with Dr. Bob and his wife at their home during the summer of 1935–the period when A.A. was founded.

But much concerning Sam Shoemaker and A.A. has taken back stage. A.A. and A.A. historians have simply ignored specifics that Sam contributed to A.A.'s Step, Big Book, and Fellowship ideas. Unless we learn those details, we will be without access to, or understanding of fundamental spiritual principles AAs borrowed from Shoemaker. One example is "finding God"–a challenge that has been distorted through lack of knowledge of its Shoemaker source.

## Basic Shoemaker Contributions

You cannot fairly appraise Sam Shoemaker's legacy to A.A. without knowing the depth and breadth of what Sam had to offer. Sam wrote over thirty books, at least half of which were circulating (before A.A.'s 12 Steps and Big Book were published in 1939) and being circulated in New York, Akron, and the Oxford Group.

Sam was also a prolific writer of sermons, pamphlets, and articles for the Calvary *Evangel*, his parish newsletter. The sermons and articles included his 1935 piece on "The Way to Find God." Also, his pamphlet on "A First Century Christian Fellowship" (the name by which the Oxford Group was known during A.A.'s formative years, and a name which Dr. Bob used to characterize Akron A.A. itself). Sam also wrote "Three Levels of Life," and "What if I Had but One Sermon to Preach" (two pamphlets which were tucked into the back of Anne Smith's Journal). Sam's booklet "One Boy's Influence" was quoted in *Anne Smith's Journal*. Six other

Shoemaker books are known for sure to have been owned, and read by, Dr. Bob and his wife Anne Smith. In all, therefore, Sam's ideas reached A.A. through his books, his pamphlets; his published sermons; his Evangel articles; his personal conversations with Bill; his influence on Bill's mentors Reverend Irving Harris, Julia Harris, Rowland Hazard, Shep Cornell, Hanford Twitchell, Victor Kitchen, and others; and Sam's actual conduct of, and leadership in, the very first alcoholic meetings on the East Coast. Meetings which were actually Oxford Group assemblages. Sam's ideas were also passed down the chute via Calvary Rescue Mission, where Bill first went for help and where he later went to find and help other drunks.

Sam Shoemaker ideas can be found in the very language of the Twelve Steps. They can be found almost verbatim in the Big Book. They are part of A.A. fellowship jargon. And they were later reiterated and explained when Shoemaker addressed A.A. International Conventions in St. Louis and subsequently at Long Beach. Also in the articles he wrote for A.A.'s *Grapevine.* Also when he wrote about A.A., as he frequently did, in his own books and pamphlets. Recall too that Sam's colleagues described him as a "Bible Christian." His books, sermons, and articles were permeated with references to the very Bible verses and chapters that became the foundation of A.A.'s own basic ideas. Principles that were studied in, and borrowed from, the Bible itself by A.A.'s Akron pioneers. Additional Shoemaker input came from Sam's frequent references to the writings of Professor William James, whom Bill Wilson was later to call a "founder" of A.A. and from whose *Varieties of Religious Experiences*, Bill obtained some significant principles. Furthermore, Sam was an outspoken advocate of Quiet Time, Bible study, prayer, and the use of devotionals; and these practices became part and parcel of early A.A. meetings, group quiet times, and personal prayer life.

Shoemaker/Wilson correspondence located at the Episcopal Church Archives in Austin, Texas also demonstrates the degree to which Wilson confided in Sam from the beginning of their friendship. The correspondence dealt with Roman Catholic influences and activities in A.A., with Oxford Group ideas, with Bill's ventures into spiritualism and LSD, and with Bill's ideas about A.A. itself.

## Specific Shoemaker Ideas in A.A.

Every AA who stays in our fellowship long enough to be exposed to its Big Book, its Twelve Steps, and its meeting buzzwords will readily recognize thoughts that seem to have come directly from the books and other writings of Sam Shoemaker.

These include: (1) Self-surrender. (2) Self is not God. (3) God either is, or He isn't. (4) "Turning point." (5) Conversion. (6) Prayer. (7) Fellowship. (8) Willingness. (9) Self-examination. (10) Confession of faults to God, self, and another. (11) Amends. (12) "Thy will be done." (13) Spiritual Experience. (14) Spiritual Awakening. (15) The unmanageable life. (16) Power greater than ourselves. (17) God as you understand Him. (18) The "Four Absolutes"-- honesty, purity, unselfishness, and love. (19) Guidance of God. (20) "Faith without works is dead." (21) "Love thy neighbor as thyself." (22) Clear references to Almighty God (using Bible terms) as our "Creator," "Maker," "Father," "Spirit," "God of our fathers," and "Father of Lights." (23) The Lord's Prayer. (24) Jesus's "sermon on the mount." (25) Self-centeredness. (26) Fear. (27) Grudges. (28) Quiet Time. (29) Reliance on God. (30) Relationship with God. (31) "Giving it away to keep it." (32) "News, not views." (33) God has a plan. (34) Seeking God first. (35) Belief in God. (36) Born again. (37) Marvel at what God has done for you. (38) Let go! (39) Abandon yourself to Him [God]. (40) "Not my will but Thine be done." And many others.

You can find, in my title *New Light on Alcoholism: God, Sam Shoemaker, and A.A.* a list of 149 Shoemaker expressions that very closely parallel A.A. language. Many more can be found in specific quotations from Shoemaker's books, books which have been fully reviewed in my New Light work on Shoemaker (http://www.dickb.com/newlight.shtml)

## Shoemaker and our Twelve Steps

Make no mistake. Whatever Bill Wilson may have said or implied from time to time, Sam Shoemaker was **not** the only source of A.A.'s spiritual ideas. Wilson often steered his applause in Sam's direction in an effort to avoid Roman Catholic and other objections to the Oxford Group from which A.A.'s ideas also came and of which early A.A. was a part. Moreover, Bill never mentioned A.A. specifics from Dr. Bob, Anne Smith, the Bible, Quiet Time, God's direct guidance or Christian literature that was daily fare in early A.A.

Remember also! Dr. Bob said he did not write the Twelve Steps and had nothing to do with writing them. Those Steps represented Bill's personal interpretation of the spiritual program that had been in progress since

1935. Dr. Bob emphasized, on more than one occasion, that A.A.'s basic ideas had come from study of the Bible. Dr. Bob studied the Bible. Daily, for three months, Anne Smith read the Bible to Bill and Bob. Dr. Bob regularly read the Bible to AAs. He quoted the Bible to AAs. He gave them Bible literature. And he frequently stressed Bible study, stating that the Book of James, 1 Corinthians 13, and Jesus's sermon on the mount (Matthew 5 to 7) were considered absolutely essential in the early spiritual recovery program. Bill Wilson and Dr. Bob both said that the sermon on the mount contained the underlying philosophy of A.A.

Nonetheless, Sam's own imprint is on the Steps–Steps that were fabricated entirely at the hand of Bill Wilson. Every one of them. Sam Shoemaker's imprint was on the presentation of Oxford Group ideas that Ebby Thacher made to Bill Wilson in Towns Hospital. And we will briefly take a look at just where Shoemaker's language parallels the language of the Twelve Steps. In fact, our third chapter in "New Light on Alcoholism" provides further details and complete documentation.

**Step One**: Shoemaker spoke of the gap between man and God which man is **powerless** to bridge, man having lost the power to deal with sin for himself. As to the **unmanageable life**, Sam referred to the prayer in the Oxford Group so often described in "Victor's Story" and quoted by Anne Smith in her journal: "God manage me, because I can't manage myself."

**Step Two**: Sam spelled out the need for a **power greater than ourselves**. He quoted Hebrews 11:6 for the proposition that **God is.** He declared: God is God, and **self is not God**; and man must so believe. Sam urged **seeking God first**, from Matthew 6:33. He espoused the "experiment of faith" by which man **believes** that God is; **seeks** God first in his actions, and then **knows** God **by doing** God's will, and seeing that God provides the needed power. For this idea, Sam frequently cited John 7:17.

**Step Three**: Sam taught about the **crisis of self-surrender as the turning point for a religious life**, quoting William James's *Varieties of Religious Experience.* Sam said it involved being **born again**; and declared that man must make a **decision** to renounce sins, **accept Jesus Christ as Saviour; and begin Christian life** in earnest. Sam illustrated a typical surrender, using language similar to that in A.A.: namely, a "decision to cast my will and my life on God." Many times, Sam said one need only surrender as much of himself as he understands to **as much of God as he understands**. A clear precursor of A.A.'s "God as we understood Him"–which has unfortunately been misunderstood and has been attributed to other sources.

**Step Four**: Sam wrote of **self-examination** to find where one's life fell short of the **Four Absolute Standards of Jesus: honesty, purity, unselfishness, and love**. One was to **write down** exactly where he had "fallen short." There was a "**moral obligation**" to face these facts, recognize these as blocks to God, and be "**ruthlessly, realistically honest**."

**Step Five**: Shoemaker taught of **honesty with self and honesty with God, quoted James 5:16 for the importance of confession to others, and stressed the need for detailed sharing of secrets**.

**Step Six**: Though the fact of Bill's borrowing of this "**conviction**" step from the Oxford Group 5 C's seems to have been overlooked, Shoemaker taught often about the need for man's conviction that he has been miserable, has (by his sins) become estranged from God, and needs to come back to God in honest penitence. Sam urged **willingness to ask God** exactly where one is failing and then to admit that sin.

**Step Seven:** Sam clarified this as the "**conversion**" step of the 5 C's. It meant a **new birth**, he said. It meant **humility**. It meant, for Shoemaker, the **assumption upon ourselves of God's will for us and the opening of ourselves to receiving the "grace of God which alone converts**." It meant "**drawing near and putting ourselves in position to be converted. . . utter dedication to the will of God**." Shoemaker often defined "sin" as that which blocks us from God and from others." So, originally, did Big Book language. And each of the foregoing life-changing steps hangs on early A.A.'s definition of sin and the "removal" process of examining for sin, confessing sin, becoming convicted of sin, and becoming converted through surrendering it to the end of being cleansed of sin nature by the power of God. The conversion experience, according to Shoemaker and early A.A., established or enabled rediscovery of a "relationship with God" and initiated the new life that developed from the relationship with God which conversion opened. Since both Wilson's Sixth and Seventh Steps were new to A.A. thinking and added something to the original "surrenders" to Jesus Christ, these Steps cannot easily be understood at all without seeing them in terms of the complete surrender, the new relationship, the new birth, and giving the sins to God, as Shoemaker saw the process and as Bill attempted to write it into the recovery path.

**Step Eight**: Wilson added this step to the Oxford Group's "restitution" idea. Bill also incorporated the Shoemaker talk of "**willingness**" to ask **God's help** in removing the blocks, being convicted of the need for restitution, and then being sent "**to someone with restoration and apology**."

**Step Nine:** Sam said the last stand of self is **pride.** There can be no talk of humility, he said, until **pride licks the dust**, and one then **acts to make full restoration and restitution for wrongs done**. As AAs in Akron did, Sam also quoted from the sermon on the mount those verses enjoining the bringing of a gift to the altar without first being reconciled to one's brother (**Matthew 5:22-24**). Restitution was not merely a good deed to be done. It was a command of God from the Bible that wrongs be righted as part of the practicing the principle of love. If one understands Shoemaker, one can understand the absurdity of some present-day AAs' guilt-ridden suggestions about writing a letter to a dead person or volunteering help for the down-trodden or making a substitutionary gift to some worthy cause. **Sam taught that the required amends were not about works. They were about love!**

**Step Ten**: This step concerned **daily surrender** and the Oxford Group idea of "**continuance**." Sam taught it was **necessary to continue** self-examination, confession, conviction, the seeking of God's help, and the prompt making of amends. This continued action was to follow the new relationship with God and others that resulted from removal of the sin problem in the earlier steps.

**Step Eleven**: Sam wrote eloquently about **Quiet Time, Bible study, prayer, and "meditation**" ("listening" for God's guidance). Sam urged daily contact with God for **guidance, forgiveness, strength, and spiritual growth**. So does A.A.'s Big Book. Quiet Time was a "must" in early A.A. And Shoemaker defined every aspect of a Quiet Time–from the necessity for a new birth to a new willingness to study, pray, listen, and read rather than to speak first and lead with the chin.

**Step Twelve**: This step comprehends: (1) **A spiritual awakening**, the exact meaning of which Shoemaker spelled out in his books and in his talks to AAs. He said spiritual awakening required conversion, prayer, fellowship, and witness. (2) **A message about what God has accomplished for us**, a phrase which Shoemaker himself used, saying, in several ways: "**You have to give Christianity away to keep it,**" said he and quite often. (3) **Practicing the new way of living in harmony with God's will and in love toward others**, an idea easily recognized from Sam's teachings that a spiritual awakening comes from conversion, that the gospel message concerns God's grace and power, and that the principles to be practiced are defined in the Bible. Accordingly, our Twelfth Step language, studied without knowledge of its Shoemaker roots, has become ill-defined and illusory. For A.A. Big Book students know that none of the three 12 Step ideas is set forth or explained in the chapter of the Big Book dealing with the Twelfth Step. To be frank, A.A. left Christianity in the dust. In so doing, AAs lost an understanding of what Sam Shoemaker taught and Dr. Bob emphasized: Conversion, the gospel message, and love and service were defined in the Book of Acts, the Four Absolutes, 1 Corinthians 13, Jesus' sermon on the mount, the Book of James, and other specific parts of the Bible.

# Appendix 3

## Miracles Not to Be Forgotten

### The Old Testament Miracles of Yahweh, the Creator

#### The Scope of Bible Miracles:

There are plenty of discussions of Old Testament signs, wonders, miracles, and healings. You can find some good ones in my bibliography. But–whatever you may think of its theology–there is one discussion that really highlights and details *all* the miracles of the Old Testament. In fact, it makes clear that the very Bible itself is a miracle whose contents were revealed to men by God. Its very contents list one miracle after another. The title is that of Dr. Herbert Lockyer: *All The Miracles of the Bible: The Supernatural in Scripture Its Scope and Significance* (Grand Rapids, Michigan: Zondervan Publishing House, 1961). Lockyer starts us off with these comments:

> A miracle has been defined as a work wrought by a divine power for a divine purpose by means beyond the reach of man. . . . Webster's definition of a miracle is clear and concise–"An event or effect in the physical world deviating from the known laws of nature, or transcending our knowledge of these laws; an extra-ordinary, anomalous, or abnormal event brought about by a super-human agency." . . . the Bible does not set itself to define miracles from the standpoint of nature or science, but from the standpoint of the moral source, the moral power, the moral aim, and the moral effect which they represented. . . . The term "miracle" then, from the Biblical standpoint is used to describe the wonderful phenomena accompanying Jewish and Christian revelations, especially at critical moments. The Biblical conception of a miracle is that of some extraordinary work of deity transcending the ordinary powers of nature and wrought in connection with the ends of revelation (pp. 13-14).

Viewed as Lockyer presents them, Bible miracles reveal the prerogative of deity to exercise almightiness in any realm. Here are some of the divisions: (1) *Power over nature* -miracles having to do with the Red Sea, Jordan, stilling storms, water into wine, walking on sea; pillar of fire, fiery furnace; Manna, feeding hundreds or thousands; thunder, floods, withered trees, opened doors. (2) *Power over disease*–provision, prevention, and permission of diseases ranging from boils, leprosy, poisonous serpents, withered hands, blindness, deafness, dumbness, lameness, infirmities. (3) *Power over death*–resurrections of Elijah's bones, the three Christ raised from the dead, the resurrection of Christ, and apostolic resurrection. (4) *Power over demons–covering* the witch at Endor, demoniacs, lunacy, unclean spirits. There are many more.

**The Common Shortcomings of Most Lists:** A few more words from Lockyer will be helpful:

> A surpassing feature of one's quest for works of profit is the fact that there is no theological treatise, at least known to the writer, dealing with *all* the miracles of the Bible. Somehow Old Testament miracles, which are as numerous, if not more so, than those found in the New Testament, are sadly neglected. . . . In several, we have scant references to some of the miracles performed by the prophets and the apostles, but a complete and comprehensive list is lacking (p, 25).
>
> Usually theological treatises dealing with Bible miracles, either for or against, omit any reference to the Bible as a miracle in itself. It is not only a Book relating credited miracles–everything associated with the Bible is miraculous. . . Everything about the Bible is supernatural, and in spite of all destructive criticism has done to weaken its authority, it remains an ever-present miracle (p. 26).

Lockyer points to the oft-ignored scope of the Bible's miracles: (1) *Miracle of its inspiration–as* originally written the Bible is wholly inspired. The divine inspiration of Scripture was the unvarying conviction of the Christian Church until the dominance of liberalism towards the close of the last century. (2) *Miracle of its antiquity–a* sacred which took some 1,500 years to complete has been in existence in its completed form for almost two millenniums. (3) *Miracle of its accuracy–Archeology*, for example, has proved to be an invaluable aid in confirming Bible records. (4) *Miracle of its harmony–Though* written by some 40 writers over 1,500 years, its 66 books agree. (5) *Miracle of its preservation.* (6) Miracle of its preparation–only a small fraction of residuary variation in the text. (7) *Miracle of its abiding power–a* triumphant ministry to a world in need.

(8) *Miracle of its circulation–still* the world's "best seller" though thousands of years old.

## A Birds Eye View of the Old Testament Miracles

We continue with Lockyer's enormous summary. You will have to do a lot of reading to cover all the miracles he points out in the Old Testament (Lockyer, *All The Miracles of the Bible*, *supra*, pp. 28-148). But here is an overview, as to which you will find Lockyer's "chapter and verse" documentation.

**The Miracles of the Books of Moses**: (1) The Miracle of Creation - of the world, of man, and the earth's development from chaos to light to firmament to dry land to vegetation to life in water and air and land, to man. (2) The Miracle of Enoch's Translation. (3) The Miracle of the Flood. (4) The Miracle of Babel. (5) The Miracle of Plagued Pharaoh. (6) The Miracle of the Smoking Furnace and Burning Lamp. (7) The Miracle of Sarah's Conception. (8) The Miracle of Blinded Sodomites and of Sodom and Gomorrah.(9) The Miracle of Lot's Wife. (10) The Miracle of Closed Wombs. (11) The Miracle of Hagar's Well. (12) The Miracle of the Burning Bush. (13) The Miracle of the Leprous Hand. (14) The Miracle of the Rod. (15) The Miracle and Miracles of Moses. (16) The Miracles of the Nile, the Frogs, the Lice, the Flies, the Murrain of Beasts, Boils and Blains, the Locusts. (17) The Miracles in Exodus as to the Darkness, Death of the Firstborn, Cloud and Fire, Red Sea. (18 The Miracles in Exodus, Leviticus, Deuteronomy, and Numbers as to the Journey, Marah's Healing Waters, Manna, Quails, Smitten Rock, Victory over Amalek, at Sinai, at Taberah, of Miriam's Leprosy, Aaron's Rod, the Brazen Serpent, of the Well, Balaam's Ass, and Moses' Death. Many of these have become so accepted and so much a part of our language that we frequently hear expressions about the Creation, the Flood, Babel, Sarah's conception, Sodom and Gomorrah, the Burning Bush, the parting of the Sea, the Journey of the children of Israel, and Manna.

**The Miracles of the Historical Books**: (1) Dividing of the Jordan. (2) Miracle Appearance. (3) Jericho. (4) Gibeon. (5) The Sun Standing Still. (6) Miracles in the Book of Judges. (7) Samson. (8) Samuel's history. (9) David's career. (10) Solomon's Reign. (11) Elijah. (12) Elisha. (13) the healings. Again, what the Bible did not directly contribute, the Negro Spirituals and Hollywood Epochs have made a part of our language and understanding.

**The Miracles in Post-Captivity Books**: Strong evidences of "God's almightiness" are to be found in the books of Ezra, Nehemiah, and Esther.

**The Miracles in the Poetical Books**: The records in Job, Psalms, Proverbs, and Ecclesiastes are loaded with pages and pages of materiel on God's providence, guidance, and deliverance.

**The Miracles in the Prophetical Books**: Prophecy is itself a miracle. The books of Isaiah, Jeremiah, Ezekiel, and Daniel–whether exemplifying miracles by the authors or testimonies to the miraculous power of God–proclaim the words of men who spoke for God and who received messages from God. Some twelve other prophetical books contain predictions of events not within human foresight, and proof that the establishment of predictions has been brought about which surpass human power and are not from man's sagacity, nor the event from man's will and design. These are Hosea, Joel, Amos, Obadiah, Jonah, Micah, Nahum, Habakkuk, Zephaniah, Haggai, Zechariah, and the concluding Malachi.

## A Focus on Healing Miracles

In Morton T. Kelsey, *Psychology, Medicine & Christian Healing*. Rev. and exp. ed. (San Francisco: Harper & Row, 1966), some very important contentions are made. Kelsey points to what he calls "some of the most touching and best-remembered stories"of Old Testament healings–accounts which we have summarized by chapter and verse below. But Kelsey contends there are two distinctly different strands pertaining to sickness and sin in the Old Testament. As to the first strand, Kelsey said:

> Health and wealth are the rewards of God, and sickness, poverty, and misfortune were divine punishments. From the beginning the law went into detail about the kind of disease Yahweh would send upon those who did not live by his covenant. . . . There is certainly no question how sickness was looked upon in this major strand of the Old Testament; it was sent by Yahweh to punish people for breaking the ritualistic or moral law (pp. 27-28).

As to the second strand, he said:

> The other strand of belief about healing found in the Old Testament is not as wide or obvious as the teaching accepted by

> Hebrew leaders. It is expressed in certain healing stories, in some of the Psalms, in the hopes of certain passages of Isaiah, and in the gigantic protest of the book of Job. This element is the one Jesus followed, the base from which he acted. As we have already seen, in the Old Testament there was no question, in theory, that Yahweh could heal. In several places remarkable instances were recorded. Some of the most touching and best-remembered stories are those in which children were given to women who were barren (p.33).

What, then, is the truth? Is Yahweh the "punishing God" we often hear mentioned by Roman Catholics in A.A. meetings–a God who visits sickness and punishment on disobedient people? Or is He the God of love, of whom Dr. Bob and his wife Anne so often spoke in early A.A.?

In *Healing: Pagan And Christian* (London: Society For Promoting Christian Knowledge, 1935), author George Gordon Dawson comments, p. 90:

> The standpoint of the Old Testament, generally, is that good health results from holy living. It is a divine gift and the reward of loving service. Any cure of disease was regarded as a gift from Yahweh, and resulted from forgiveness. The sick person made his peace with Him by repentance, intercession, and sacrifice. The right spiritual relationship was restored. The soul was at rest, and the inner life being calm the bodily symptoms disappeared.

Alan Richardson wrote at pp. 3-4:

> . . . [I]n the Old Testament the historically decisive event, which became for the Hebrew mind, the symbol and type of all God's comings in history is the Miracle of the Red Sea. *The Miracle Stories of the Gospels* (London: SCM Press Ltd., 1941).

Again, what is the truth? A God of wrath, punishment, and justice? A God of love, forgiveness, and salvation? To answer could provide you with volumes of commentaries and opinions.

On the foregoing issues, we'd prefer to pass and to move away from statements and observations of commentators. Let's look at the Bible itself.

## First, the Specific Examples of Healing

**Children given to women who were barren** (Genesis 18:10, Judges 13:5, 24; 1 Samuel 1:19-20; 2 Kings 4:16-17).

**The healing of Miriam's leprosy and Naaman's leprosy** (Numbers 12:1-15; 2 Kings 5:1-14).

**The healing of Jeroboam's paralyzed hand** (1 Kings 13:1-6).

**Raising from the dead by Elijah and by Elisha** (1 Kings 17:17-24; 2 Kings 4:1-37).

**Salvation of the Israelites from the later plagues in Egypt** (Numbers 21:6-9).

**Miracles wrought by Moses** (Exodus 7 - 17).

For summaries, see *New Bible Dictionary, Second Edition* (England: Inter-Varsity Press, 1982), pp. 457-65; Kelsey, *Psychology, Medicine, & Christian Healing, supra,* pp. 35-36; Lockyer, All *The Miracles of The Bible*, *supra*, pp. 25-148.

## Second, Some Old Testament Bible Verses to Study

**Exodus 15:26:**

> And [Yahweh] said, If thou wilt diligently hearken to the voice of the LORD [Yahweh] thy God, and wilt do that which is right in his sight, and will give ear to his commandments, and keep all his statutes, I will put none of these diseases upon thee, which I have brought upon the Egyptians; for I *am* the LORD [Yahweh] that healeth thee.

**Deuteronomy 4:29-31**:

> But if from thence thou shall seek the Lord thy God, thou shalt find *him*, if thou seek him with all thy heart and with all thy soul. When thou art in tribulation, and all these things are come upon thee, *even* in the latter days, if thou turn to the Lord thy God, and shalt be obedient unto his voice; (For the Lord thy

God *is* a merciful God;) he will not forsake thee, neither destroy thee, nor forget the covenant of thy fathers which he sware unto them.

**Deuteronomy 4:39-40:**

Know therefore this day, and consider it in thine heart, that the Lord he *is* God in heaven above, and upon the earth beneath: *there is* none else. Thou shalt keep therefore his statutes, and his commandments which I command thee this day, that it may go well with thee, and with thy children after thee, and that thou mayest prolong *thy* days upon the earth, which the Lord thy God giveth thee, for ever.

**Deuteronomy 7:8-9, 11-15:**

But because the Lord loved you, and because he would keep the oath which he had sworn unto your fathers, hath the Lord brought you out with a mighty hand, and redeemed you out of the house of bondsmen, from the hand of Pharaoh king of Egypt. Know therefore that the Lord thy God, he *is* God, the faithful God, which keepeth covenant and mercy with them that love him and keep his commandments to a thousand generations.

Thou shalt therefore keep the commandments, and the statutes, and the judgments, which I command me this day, to do them. Wherefore it shall come to pass, if ye hearken to these judgments, and keep and do them, that the Lord thy God shall keep unto thee the covenant and the mercy which he sware unto thy fathers. And he will love thee, and bless thee, and multiply thee: he will also bless the fruit of thy womb, and the fruit of thy land, thy corn, and thy wine, and thine oil, the increase of thy kine, and the flocks of thy sheep, in the land which he sware unto the fathers to give thee. Thou shalt be blessed above all people. . . . And the Lord will take away from thee all sickness, and will put none of the evil diseases of Egypt which thou knowest, upon thee; but will lay them upon all *them* that hate thee.

**Psalm 103:2-3**:

Bless the Lord, O my soul, and forget not all his benefits. Who forgiveth all thine iniquities; who healeth all thy diseases; Who redeemeth thy life from destruction; who crowneth thee with lovingkindness and tender mercies.

**Psalm 107:9-20**:

> Then they cry unto the Lord in their trouble, *and* he saveth them out of their distresses. He sent his word, and healed them, and *delivered* them from their destructions.

**Psalm 91:11-16**:

> For he shall give his angels charge over thee, to keep thee in all thy ways. They shall bear thee up in *their* hands, lest thou dash thy foot against a stone. Thou shalt tread upon the lion and adder; the young lion and the dragon shalt thou trample under feet. Because he hath set his love upon me, therefore will I deliver him: I will set him on high, because he hath known my name. He shall call upon me, and I will answer him: I *will be* with him in trouble; I will deliver him, and honor him. With long life will I satisfy him, and shew him my salvation.

The Word of God, as it is set forth in the Old Testament, tells us that Yahweh has given us commandments and statutes. He commands us to obey them. It tells us He loves us, forgives us, heals our diseases, redeems our lives from destruction, and crowns us with lovingkindness and tender mercies. It tells us we can cry out to him in trouble and be saved from our distresses, be healed of our diseases, and be delivered from destructions. He will guide us. He will protect us. He will not forsake us if we obey Him.

We've included lots on Old Testament miracles because many seem to think that, if you mention God, healing, cure, and so on that you are dealing with "the Christian God" or "Christian Bible." But the fact is that the Bible is the Bible is the Bible–however many manuscripts, canons, translations, and versions may have contributed to its content. And the Old Testament is testimony to what God can do and has done long before the birth of His son Jesus Christ and of the Christian church described in the Book of Acts and thereafter. The materials sketched from here on have been covered in detail elsewhere and will be covered in future materials. But they establish that healing and cures by the power of God are not something dreamed up in 1935 by Bible thumpers from Akron

## The Gospels

Straight from the Bible, we are told as to Jesus: "they brought unto Him all that were sick and them that were possessed with demons, and He healed many that were sick with divers diseases, and cast out many demons. . . He had healed many in so much that as many as had plagues pressed upon Him that they might touch Him." See Elwood Worcester, Samuel McComb, Isador H. Coriat, *Religion and Medicine* (NY: Moffat, Yard & Company, 1908), p. 3 45; Elwood Worcester and Samuel McComb, *The Christian Religion As A Healing Power* (NY: Moffat, Yard & Company, 1909), pp. 84-97; G. R. H. Shafto, *The Wonders of The Kingdom: A Study of the Miracles of Jesus* (NY: George H. Doran Company, 1942), pp. 8-9. Shafto concluded that there are some forty-two of the foregoing indirect references to the miraculous action on the part of Jesus in the four Gospels.

Kelsey concluded: ". . . we find that everywhere Jesus went he functioned as a religious healer. Forty-one instances of physical and mental healing are recorded in the four gospels (there are seventy-two accounts in all, including duplications), but this by no means represents the total. Many of these references summarize the healings of large numbers of people. See Morton T. Kelsey, *Psychology, Medicine, and Christian Healing*, Rev. and exp ed. (San Francisco: Harper & Row, Publishers, 1966), pp. 42-47. Alan Richardson points out the high proportion of the Gospel tradition that is devoted to the subject of miracle (209 verses out of 666 in the Gospel of Mark). See Richardson, *The Miracle Stories of the Gospels*, *supra*, p. 36.

There are over 20 specific accounts–some healed at a distance, some with a word, and some with physical contact and means: blindness, deafness, dumbness, leprosy, epilepsy, dropsy, uterine hemorrhage, Peter's mother-in-law and her fever–possibly malaria, Malchus' severed ear, the man with withered hand, the woman bent double with a "spirit of infirmity," three separate people resurrected from the dead, the man paralyzed for 38 years, demoniacal possession, and so on. Pearcy Dearmer reports there are forty-one instances of Christ's works of healing in the Gospels. See Pearcy Dearmer, *Body and Soul: An Enquiry into the Effects of Religion upon Health, with a Description of Christian Works of Healing From the New Testament to the Present Day* (London: Sir Isaac Pitman & Sons, Ltd., 1909), pp. 142-146.

There were also the miracles of water converted to wine, stilling of a storm, supernatural catch of fish, multiplying food, walking on water, money from a fish, and a fig tree dried up. See *New Bible Dictionary, Second Edition* (England: Inter-Varsity Press, 1982), pp. 462-463; Leslie D. Weatherhead, *Psychology, Religion and Healing* (NY: Abingdon-Cokesbury Press, 1951, pp. 29-69; Worcester, McComb, Coriat, *Religion and Medicine, supra*, pp. 338-368; Josh McDowell, *Evidence That Demands a Verdict: Historical Evidences for the Christian Faith* (Campus Crusade for Christ, 1973), pp. 128-131.

The Gospel healings and miracles brought about by Jesus are summarized in Luke:

> Luke 7:21-22:
> And in that same hour he cured many of their infirmities and plagues, and of evil spirits; and unto many that were blind he gave sight. Then Jesus answering said unto them, Go your way. and tell John what things ye have seen and heard; how that the blind see, the lame walk, the lepers are cleansed, the deaf hear, the dead are raised, to the poor the gospel is preached.

For a survey of the evidence, see E. R. Micklem, *Miracles & The New Psychology: A Study in the Healing Miracles of the New Testament* (London: Oxford University Press, 1922).

## The Book of Acts in Apostolic Times

Straight from the Bible, we are told as to the Apostles: "many wonders and signs were done by the apostles. . . by the hands of the apostles were many signs and wonders wrought among the people. . . . Stephen, full of grace and power, wrought great wonders and signs. . . [as to Philip in Samaria] many with unclean spirits and many that were palsied and lame. . . [as to Paul and Barnabus] speaking of the signs and wonders God wrought among the gentiles by them. . . [as to healing activities of Paul on the island of Malta] The rest also who had diseases in the island came and were cured." See Weatherhead, *Psychology, Religion, and Healing, supra*, pp. 70-72; Kelsey, *Psychology, Medicine and Christian Healing, supra,* pp. 83-102.

In addition to the general descriptions, there are, of course, many specific descriptions of healings and cures: the lame man at the Gate Beautiful, patients cured by the shadow of Peter and handkerchiefs which had touched them; restoration of the sight of Saul by Ananias; Peter's healing Aenes of palsy; the paralytic healed by Paul at Lystra; the healing of Publius's father of fever and dysentery by Paul; Dorcas and Eutychus raised from the dead; multiple healings; and two occasions where demons were cast out. See *New Bible Dictionary*, *supra*, pp. 462-464.

Harnack summed up these miraculous cures by quoting the following from Hebrews 2:3-4:

> How shall we escape, if we neglect so great salvation: which at the first began to be spoken by the Lord, and was confirmed unto us by them that heard him; God also bearing witness, both with signs and winders, and with divers miracles, and gifts of the Holy Ghost, according to his own will? See Adolph Harnack, *The Expansion of Christianity in the First Three Centuries*, Vol I (Eugene, OR: Wpf and Stock Publishers, 1998), pp. 250-73.

There are several specific lists of miracles in the Acts of the Apostles. See Dearmer, *Body and Soul*, *supra*, pp. 183-191.

## Christian Healings After Apostolic Times and in Early Centuries

Many many writers have blotched the Christian healing scene with the assertion that the "Age of Miracles" somehow left us centuries ago. Various theories allege that God no longer needed them, that the Church ignored them, or that somehow they just did not occur. The Oxford Group itself fostered this belief by claiming that for them, "The Age of Miracles has returned." But to support such claims, one has to ignore century after century of history to the contrary. As we'll show, there have been many writings that show the real picture. One of the most comprehensive is set forth in Roberts Liardon's *John G. Lake*: *The Complete Collection of His Life Teachings* (Tulsa, OK: Albury Publishing, 1999. That treatise and other works cited below show strong evidence of Christian healings from these sources:

> Quadratus of Athens (AD 126 or 127); St. Justin Martyr (the philosopher martyred circa 163–AD 100-163); St. Iranaeus (Bishop of Lyons, AD 120-202); Origin of Alexandria (AD 185-253); Tertullian (AD 193-211); St. Hilarion (monk, AD 291-371); St. Parthenius (Bishop of Lampsacus, AD circa 335-355); St. Ambrose (Bishop of Milan, 340-397 AD); St.

> Macarius of Alexandra and four other monks (AD 340-397); St. Chrysostom (AD 347-4 07); St. Augustine (AD 354-430); St. Jerome (AD 340-420); St. Symeon Sylites (layman, AD 391-460); St. Eugendus, Abbot of a monastery near Geneva, AD 45 5-517); St. Caesarius (Bishop of Arles, 502-542); St. German (Bishop of Paris, circa AD 555-576); St. Laumer (priest near Chartres, AD 548-651); St. Eustace (Abbot of Luxeuil, circa AD 624-6 25); St. Riemirus (abbot of a monastery in the diocese of Le Mans, circa 660-699); Sophronius (Patriarch of Jerusalem, AD 640); St. Cuthbert (Bishop of Lindisfarne, AD 635-657; and St. John of Beverley (by Bede, AD 721).

See Weatherhead, *Psychology, Religion, and Healing*, *supra*, pp. 76 -84; Worcestler, McComb, and Coriat, *Religion and Medicine*, *supra*, p. 367; Worcester and McComb, *The Christian Religion*, *supra*, p. 367. Then, in a monumental treatise, based largely on the Book of James as it relates to healing and anointing, F. W. Puller declares:

> I think I have shown that from the time of the Apostles onwards, during the first seven centuries of our era, the custom of praying over sick people and anointing them with holy oil continued without any break. And there seems to me to be good reasons for believing that in many cases the petitions that were offered were granted and that the holy oil was used by God as a channel for conveying health to sick persons (See F. W. Puller, *The Anointing of the Sick in Scripture and Tradition, with some Considerations on the Numbering of the Sacraments*. London: Society For Promoting Christian Knowledge, 1904, p. 188).

Evelyn Frost made a study of the earliest records of the church after the New Testament, from about 100-250. See Frost, *Christian Healing: A Consideration of the Place of Spiritual Healing in the Church Today in the Light of the Doctrine and Practice of the Ante-Nicene Church*, 1940. Kelsey says of the Frost study: "It shows clearly that the practices of healing described in the New Testament continued without interruption for the next two centuries." Kelsey, *Psychology, Medicine and Christian Healing*, *supra*, pp. 103-156.

## Individual Healing Ministries from 1091 to the Early 1800's

John Lake, among many others, says that, among those canonized, and others, in whose lives was positive evidence of the healing power of Christ in well-established cases, are:

> St. Bernard (AD 1091-1153); St. Francis of Assisi (AD 1182-1226); St. Thomas of Hereford (AD 1282-1303); St. Catherine of Siena (AD 1347-1380); Martin Luther (AD 1483-1546); St. Francis of Xavier (AD 1506-1552); St. Philip Neri (AD 1515-1595); Pascal's niece (AD 1646); George Fox (AD 16 24-1691); John Wesley (AD 1703-1791); Prince Alexander of Hohenlohe (1794-1847); Father Theobald Matthew (of Ireland, AD 1790-1856); Dorothea Trudel (from Zurich, AD 1813-1862); Pastor John Christopher Blumhardt (Lutheran Pastor from Stuttgart, AD 1805-1880); and Father John of Cronstadt (of the Orthodox Church of the East, AD 1829-1908).

See Liardon, *John G. Lake*, *supra*, pp. 690-695.;Weatherhead, *supra,* p. 86; Worcester and McComb, *supra*, p. 367; Dearmer, *supra*, pp. 278, 338-382; Kelsey, *supra*, pp. 157-188.

## The Christian Healing Scene From 1800 Forward

I'll leave to another time and another study the story of the dynamic healers of the last two centuries. But it always amuses me to see how the revisionist, detour writers today focus on the failed Washingtonians and the Emmanuel Movement's psychological work and ignore two centuries of astonishingly effective individual Christian healers and healings. You can find plenty of material slamming the healing people, but you need to cut through the negatives and look at the records. You need to read the hundreds of eye witness accounts of healings. Decide for yourself, and forget Wilson's Washingtonian and Emmanuel diversions. What have they to do with the cures reported by A.A. people in the 1930's and early 1940's when A.A. pioneers truly relied on Divine Aid, as they put it.

### The Real Christian Healers

Some informative reviews can be found in Roberts Lairdon, *God's Generals: Why They Succeeded and Why They Failed* (Tulsa, OK: Albury Publishing, 1996). The following are the people Lairdon covers. Their huge efforts and, on many occasions, healing successes make fascinating reading for one who thinks an alcoholic cannot be cured by God. They are, as Lairdon describes them:

John Alexander Dowie, "The Healing Apostle;" Maria Woodworth-Etter, "Demonstrator of the Spirit;" Evan Roberts, "Welsh Revivalist;" Charles Fox Parham, "The Father of Pentecost;" William J. Seymour, "The Catalyst of Pentecost;" John G. Lake, "A Man of Healing;" Smith Wigglesworth, "Apostle of Faith;" Aimee Semple McPherson, "A Woman of Destiny;" Kathryn Kuhlman, "The Woman Who Believed in Miracles;" William Branham, "A Man of Notable Signs and Wonders;" Jack Coe, "The Man of Reckless Faith; and A.A. Allen, "The Miracle Man."

The healings these people accomplished are parallel to those described in the Old Testament, the Gospels, the Book of Acts, and the Christian healings through the centuries. Read and decide!

The books by and about these Christians provide top notch reading for today's A.A. and Twelve Step members. They demonstrate the power of God, His promises of healing, and the reliability of believing His word and words about healing, and of what Christ accomplished that makes it possible for believers. See also Liardon, *John G. Lake*, *supra*, pp. 690-712. Biographies and autobiographies of the foregoing are included in my bibliography of this title.

**Today's Powerful Healing Books and the Healers Who Wrote Them**

There are many other healers who should survive the cut when it comes to selecting successful healers for study. Some of these people held huge tent meetings where hundreds of thousands of people were healed around the world. There are photographs and movies of the meetings, of the huge crowds, and of the healings. Specific statements as to who was healed and where, and the repercussions of their beliefs and cures in entire communities. Some of the Christian healers were studied by Dr. Bob himself. Some are still in motion. Some are teachers. Many have been criticized. But all contribute one way or another to the case for healing by the power of God–a healing sought and received by early AAs and embodied in their early program. Here are some of the names, and you can find their autobiographies or biographies in my bibliography:

James Moore Hickson, Ethel R. Willitts, Oral Roberts, T. L. Osborn, E.W. Kenyon, F. F. Bosworth, Thomas Wyatt, A.B. Simpson, Andrew Murray, R. Kelso-Carter, William Boardman, Raymond T. Richey, Gordon Lindsay, Stephen Jeffrys, Charles Price, O. L. Jaggers, Gayle Jackson, Velmer Gardner, Richard

Vineyard, Richard Jeffries, W.V. Grant, Sr., Neal Frisby, C. S. Lovett, Charles Cullis, and Pat Robertson.

There is no assertion that this or that person among the foregoing was or is right or wrong, successful or unsuccessful, stayed on the path or strayed, or shared the same view as the others. To their names could be added those of Glenn Clark, Mary Baker Eddy, A.J. Gordon, Pearcy Dearmer, Agnes Sanford, Starr Daily, John and Ethel Banks, Ruth Carter Stapleton, and a number in the Roman Catholic Community. See Kelsey, *Psychology, Medicine and Christian Religion, supra*, pp. 186-184. Read for yourself and decide. Read, just as Dr. Bob and the early pioneers did. Why waste time with the resentments and utterances at meetings, slamming religion, slamming the Bible, slamming God, slamming Jesus Christ. And slamming you if you open your mouth. The remarkable people listed here are simply those who appear to have taken God at His word. They preached Scriptures that said, for example, "By his stripes, we were healed." They contended that the key was believing God, rejecting senses knowledge perceptions that there was or could be no healing, and walking out on God's word. Healed. Just as A.A. Number Three was healed. There is very little difference between the verses and teachings of these people and those that could be found in the basic verses Dr. Bob and early pioneers studied in the Bible itself and in *The Runner's Bible*.

**Don't forget the Salvation Army, the Gospel Missions, Lourdes, the Oxford Group, Teen Challenge, A.A.'s Own Believer Retreats and Conferences, and all the others**

There are plenty of Christian groups (other than the early Alcoholics Anonymous Christian Fellowship), and more than you may realize *inside* Alcoholics Anonymous, that have brought people to Christ, taught them Scripture, urged them to believe what God could do for them, and seen the wretched cured. Certainly that was the essence of our founding Akron meetings. All these reinforce the proofs that alcoholism can be cured and has been cured by the power of God when the Word of God is believed.

Just think. Healings by the power of God. No government subsidies. No insurance coverage. No dues or fees. No budgets. No rehabs. No treatment centers. No treatment professionals. Just ambassadors for Christ doing what Jesus said they could do. For years and years and years.

**Some Major Promises of God**

Yahweh's promises and assurances in His Word have not changed. See:

> Exodus 15:26: "I am the Lord [Yahweh in the texts] that healeth thee;"
>
> Psalm 103:3-4: Who [Yahweh our God] forgives all our iniquities, heals all our diseases, and redeems our lives from destruction.
>
> Matthew 10:8: "Heal the sick, cleanse the lepers, raise the deed, cast out devils; freely ye have received, freely give."
>
> Mark 16:19-20: "And these signs shall follow them that believe: In my name shall they cast out devils; they shall speak with new tongues. . . they shall lay hands on the sick, and they shall recover."
>
> John 14:12: "Verily, verily, I say unto you, He that believeth on me, the works that I do shall he do also; and greater works than these shall he do; because I go unto my Father."

These and many other assurances that we can heal and be healed through the power of God were the daily diet of many early A.A. pioneers, and particularly Dr. Bob as he frequently used *The Runner's Bible* for devotional and study purposes. Read and see for yourself.

For the relevance to your own cure of the foregoing verses and many others in the Bible, see Nora Smith Holm, *The Runner's Bible: Spiritual Guidance for People On the Run* (Lakewood, CO: I-Level Acropolis Books, Publisher, 1998), pp. 171-196; A. J. Pridie, *The Church's Ministry of Healing* (London: Society For Promoting Christian Knowledge, 1926); C.S. Lewis, *Miracles: How God Intervenes in Nature and Human Affairs* (NY: Collier Books, 1947); Friedrich Heiler, *Prayer: A Study in the History of Psychology and Religion* (Oxford: Oneworld, 1932); Jim Wilson, *Healing Through the Power of Christ* (Cambridge: James Clarke & Co., Ltd., 1946); Dawson, *Healing: Pagan and Christian*, 1935, *supra*; Philip Inman, *Christ in the Modern Hospital* (London: Hodder & Stoughton, Limited, 1937); G. R.H. Shafto, *The Wonders of the Kingdom*, 1924, *supra*; T. L. Osborn, *Healing The Sick* (Tulsa, OK: Harrison House, 1992); R.W. Schambach, *The Price of God's Miracle-Working Power* (TX: Schambach Ministries, Inc., 1991); E. W. Kenyon, *Jesus the Healer* (Kenyon's Gospel Publishing Society, 2000); Norvel Hayes, *The Healing Handbook* (Tulsa, OK: Harrison House, 1982); Ron McIntosh, *The Quest for Revival*, Tulsa, OK: Harrison House, 1997; Smith

Wigglesworth, *Smith Wigglesworth on Healing*. PA; Whitaker House, 1999.

Treat yourselves to these books. See what the writers saw. See what the healers did. See what they suggest as to prayer, Scripture, and believing. I've watched people in A.A. pray for others in an A.A. meeting. They knew what God said as to healing. They knew what Jesus said as to prayer. They knew the appropriate Scriptures. They knew the appropriate prayers. They believed, And, with the power of God, they healed. I've been there. I've participated. I've seen. Believers have the power and can use it. Read the Book of Acts as Anne Ripley Smith, Dr. Bob's wife, suggested. Then decide for yourself.

# Appendix 4

## For A.A. Pioneers, Alcoholism Was Curable and Cured

Author and A.A. historian Richard K. has assembled a large number of materials on the many who claimed cure and the many who reported that people could be and had been cured at the time of early A.A. These materials are available for presentation at nationwide history conferences and will be in book form shortly. The title–taken from a headline in 1941 article in a World Services scrapbook–is *So You Think Drunks Can't Be Cured?*

There is neither the time nor place here to list the hundreds of times the absolute cure of drunks was claimed and mentioned in the early A.A. days. Richard K. and I were elated as we went through some of them from the Yale Lectures, from A.A. General Services, and from the remarks of old timers.

I wish the President of the United States, his Drug Czar, his Health and Human Services Secretary, and all the people drawing grant money for research could be persuaded to look at the testimonies about early A.A. They just don't seem to have seen them, discussed them, or considered them.

Perhaps the most shocking and revolting example of the revisionism in A.A. itself is the fabrication perpetrated with the famous Elrick Davis articles in the *Cleveland Plain Dealer*. The situation is covered in Richard K.'s *A.A.-Separating Fact From Fiction*, *supra.* As the newspaper writer originally wrote the material, it was loaded with references to the "cures" to "cured" and to the testimonies of "cure." It appeared that way in the well-known series of news articles themselves. Yet, when it was republished by A.A. people in A.A. itself, every single one of those references was deleted and replaced with language compatible with the later-fabricated "no cure" and "once an alcoholic, always an alcoholic" doctrine of hopelessness.

The great majority of people interested in recovery, including A.A. members, don't have an inkling of the treacherous editing that has deleted "cure" from newspaper articles and pamphlets and replaced it with terms more acceptable to the revisionist heirarchy.

The only clue that amounts to an admission of this same presumptuous and disgusting revision was inserted by the writer of *DR. BOB and the Good Oldtimers* where his remarks all but called the following liars: Bill Wilson, Dr. Bob, Bill Dotson, Frank Amos, A.A. trustees, the physicians Silkworth and Tiebout, and the writers of the 1930's. The A.A. staff writer's remarks should be stricken from A.A. literature as an abomination. And, until this kind of wholesale house-cleaning takes place, A.A. members will continue in meetings to condemn those healthy souls who know and say they believe in God, study the Bible, are Christians, and have been cured by the power of God. I've been subjected to that kind of outspoken criticism. Sometimes the critics operate with undercover criticism–namely the banning of books, the outrageous appeal to admirers of Ignatia and Dowling by saying I exclude them from history, and the censorship of submissions to websites by prejudiced "moderators." Many I have sponsored have been in that same position. And I am receiving hundreds of letters and emails and phone calls from all over the world coming from people receiving and disgusted with like outbursts. The uncontrolled outbursts just aren't A.A. They're uncontrolled sickness.

# Bibliography


*Alcoholics Anonymous.* New Jersey: Works Publishing Company, 1939 [the "First Edition"]

*Alcoholics Anonymous*, 4th ed. NY: Alcoholics Anonymous World Services, Inc., 2002.

*Alcoholics Anonymous Comes of Age.* NY: Alcoholics Anonymous World Services, Inc., 1957.

Alexander, William Menzies. *Demonic Possession in the New Testament: Its Historical, Medical, and Theological Aspects.* Grand Rapids: Baker Book House, 1980.

*A Guide to the Twelve Steps of Alcoholics Anonymous.* Akron: AA of Akron, n.d.

*A Manual for Alcoholics Anonymous*, rev. ed. AA of Akron, 1989

*AA Grapevine, The*: "RHS" - issue dedicated to the memory of the Co-Founder of Alcoholics Anonymous, DR. BOB. NY: The AA Grapevine, Inc., 1951.

Allen, A. A. *How To Have Power Over The Devil.* AZ: A. A. Allen Revivals, Inc., 1954.

_____. *My Cross*. TX: A.A. Allen Revivals, Inc., n.d.

Allen, James. *As a Man Thinketh.* NY: Peter Pauper Press, Inc., n.d.

Anderson, Bernard W. *Understanding The Old Testament.* NJ: Prentice Hall, 1957.

*A Newcomer Asks. . .* York, England: A.A. Sterling Area Services, n.d.

B., Dick. *Anne Smith's Journal, 1933-1939*, 3rd ed. Kihei, HI: Paradise Research Publications, Inc., 1998

_____. *By the Power of God: A Guide to Early A.A. Groups & Similar Groups Today.* Kihei, HI: Paradise Research Publications, Inc., 2000.

_____. *Cured!: Proven Help for Alcoholics and Addicts.* Kihei, HI: Paradise Research Publications, Inc., 2003.

_____. *Dr. Bob and His Library*, 3rd ed., Kihei, HI: Paradise Research Publications, Inc., 1998

_____. *God and Alcoholism: Our Growing Opportunity in the 21st Century.* Kihei, HI: Paradise Research Publications, Inc., 2002.

_____. *Good Morning!: Quiet Time, Morning Watch, Meditation, and Early A.A.*, 2d ed. Kihei, HI: Paradise Research Publications, Inc., 1998.

_____. *Henrietta Seiberling: Ohio's Lady with a Cause*. Kihei, HI: Paradise Research Publications, Inc., 2004.

_____. *Making Known the Biblical History and Roots of Alcoholics Anonymous.* Kihei, HI: Paradise Research Publications, Inc., 2001.

_____. *New Light on Alcoholism: God, Sam Shoemaker, and A.A.*, 2d ed. Kihei, HI: Paradise Research Publications, Inc., 1999.

_____. *The Akron Genesis of Alcoholics Anonymous*, 2d ed. Kihei, HI: Paradise Research Publications, Inc., 1998.

_____. *The Books Early AAs Read for Spiritual Growth*, 7th ed. Kihei, HI: Paradise Research Publications, Inc., 1998.

_____. *The Golden Text of A.A.: God, the Pioneers, and Real Spirituality*. Kihei, HI: Paradise Research Publications, Inc., 1999.
_____. *The Good Book and The Big Book: A.A.'s Roots in the Bible*, 2d ed. Kihei, HI: Paradise Research Publications, Inc., 1997.
_____. *The Oxford Group and Alcoholics Anonymous*, 2d ed. Kihei, HI: Paradise Research Publications, Inc., 1998.
_____. *That Amazing Grace* (Clarence & Grace S.). Kihei, HI: Paradise Research Publications, Inc., 1996.
_____. *Turning Point: A History of Early A.A.'s Spiritual Roots and Successes.* Kihei, HI: Paradise Research Publications, Inc., 1997.
_____. *Twelve Steps for You* (Kihei, HI: Paradise Research Publications, Inc., 2003)
_____. *Utilizing Early A.A.'s Spiritual Roots for Recovery Today*, Rev. ed. Kihei, HI: Paradise Research Publications, Inc., 1999.
_____. *Why Early A.A. Succeeded: The Good Book in Alcoholics Anonymous Yesterday and Today (A Bible Study Primer*). Kihei, HI: Paradise Research Publications, Inc., 2001.
B., Mel. *New Wine: The Spiritual Roots of the Twelve Step Miracle.* Hazelden, 1991.
_____. *Ebby: The Man Who Sponsored Bill W.* MN: Hazelden, 1998.
Barton, Bruce. *The Man Nobody Knows: A Discovery of the Real Jesus*. IN: Bobbs-Merrill, 1925.
Begbie, Harold. *Life Changers*. NY: G. P. Putnam's Sons, 1927.
_____. *Twice Born Men.* NY: Fleming H. Revell, 1909.
*Best of the Grapevine, Volume II.* NY: The AA Grapevine, Inc., 1986.
Bobgan, Martin and Deidre. *12 Steps to Destruction: Codependency Recovery Heresies.* Santa Barbara, CA: EastGate Publishers, 1991.
Bosworth, F. F. *Christ The Healer*. MI: Fleming H. Revell, 1996.
Brown, Kenneth O. *Holy Ground, Too: The Camp Meeting Family Tree.* PA: Holiness Archives, 1997.
Brown, William. *Personality and Religion.* London: University of London Press, Ltd., 1946.
Bruns, Roger A. *Preacher Billy Sunday and Big-Time American Evangelism*. Urbana: University of Illinois Press, 1992.
Burns, Dr. Cathy. *Alcoholics Anonymous Unmasked: Deception and Deliverance*. Mt. Carmel, PA: Sharing, 1991.
Bushnell, Horace. *The New Life.* London: Strahan & Co., 1868.
C., Stewart. *A Reference Guide to the Big Book of Alcoholics Anonymous*. Seattle: Recovery Press, 1986.
Cabot, Richard C. and Russell L. Dicks. *The Art of Ministering to the Sick.* NY: The Macmillan Company, 1946.
Chambers, Oswald. *My Utmost for His Highest.* Oswald Chambers Publishing Assn., 1963.
_____. *Studies in the Sermon on the Mount.* MI: Discovery House, 1960.
Clapp, Charles, Jr. *The Big Bender*. NY: Harper & Row, 1938.
Clark, Francis E. *Christian Endeavor in All Lands.* N.p.: The United Society of Christian Endeavor, 1906.
_____. *Memoirs of Many Men in Many Lands: An Autobiography*. Boston: United Society of Christian Endeavor, 1922.
Clark, Glenn. *How to Find Health Through Prayer*. NY: Harper & Row, 1940.
*Cleveland Central Bulletin.* Volumes I - III Cleveland Central Committee, Oct/42 - Dec/45.

Clinebell, Howard. *Understanding and Counseling Persons with Alcohol, Drug, and Behavioral Addictions.* Rev. and enl. ed. Nashville: Abingdon Press, 1998.
*Comparative Study Bible.* Rev ed. MI: Zondervan Publishing House, 1999.
*Complete Jewish Bible.* Clarksville, MD: Jewish New Testament Publications, Inc., 1998.
Daily, Starr. *Recovery.* Minnesota: Macalester Park Publishing, 1948.
_____. *Release.* NY : Harper & Brothers, 1942
Darrah, Mary C. *Sister Ignatia: Angel of Alcoholics Anonymous.* Chicago: Loyola University Press, 1992.
Dawson, George Gordon. *Healing: Pagan and Christian.* London: Society For Promoting Christian Knowledge, 1935.
Day, Sherwood Sunderland. *The Principles of the Group.* Oxford: University Press, n.d.
Dearmer, Percy. *Body and Soul: An Enquiry into the Effects of Religion Upon Health, With a Description of Christian Works of Healing From the New Testament to the Present Day.* London: Sir Isaac Pitman & Sons, Ltd., 1909.
*DR. BOB and the Good Oldtimers.* NY: Alcoholics Anonymous World Services, Inc., 1980.
Drummond, Henry. *The Greatest Thing in the World.* Fleming H. Revell, 1968.
_____. *The Ideal Life.* NY: Dodd, Mead and Company, 1898.
Dunn, Jerry. *God is for the Alcoholic.* Chicago: Moody Press, 1965.
E., Bob. *Handwritten Note to Lois Wilson on pamphlet entitled "Four Absolutes."* (Copy made available to author by Founders Day Archivist, Akron, Ohio, in June, 1991)
_____. Letter from Bob E. to Nell Wing. NY: Stepping Stones Archives, Bedford Hills, NY.
Eddy, Mary Baker. *Science and Health with Key to the Scriptures.* Boston: Published by the Trustees under the Will of Mary Baker Eddy, 1916.
Ellis, William T. *Billy Sunday: The Man and His Message.* Chicago: Moody Press, 1959.
Fillmore, Charles. *Christian Healing.* Kansas City: Unity School of Christianity, 1936.
Fillmore, Charles and Cora. *Teach Us to Pray.* MO: Unity School of Christianity, 1945.
Forde, Eleanor Napier. *Guidance: What It Is and How to Get It.* Paper presented by Eleanor Napier Forde at Minnewaska, New York, September, 1927.
_____. *The Guidance of God.* London: The Oxford Group, 1927.
Fosdick, Harry Emerson. *The Man from Nazareth: As His Contemporaries Saw Him.* NY: Harper & Brothers, 1949.
_____. *The Meaning of Prayer.* NY: Association Press, 1915.
Fox, Emmet. *Find and Use Your Inner Power.* NY: Harper & Brothers, 1937.
_____. *Getting Results by Prayer* (pamphlet, 1933).
_____. *Power through Constructive Thinking.* NY: Harper & Brothers, 1932.
_____. *The Sermon on the Mount.* New York: Harper & Row, 1934.
Frame, Hugh F. *Wonderful, Counsellor: A Study in the Life of Jesus.* London: Hodder And Stoughton Limited, 1935.
Frost, Evelyn. *Christian Healing: A Consideration of the Place of Spiritual Healing in the Church of To-day in the Light of the Doctrine and Practice of the Ante-Nicene Church.* London: A.R. Mobray & Co. Limited, 1940.

Gilkey, Charles Whitney. *Jesus and Our Generation*. Chicago: The University of Chicago Press, 1925.

Glover, T. R. *The Jesus of History*. New York: Association Press, 1930.

Grant, W. V. *Just Before The Healing Service.* TX: Faith Clinic, n.d.

_____. *Live all Your Life.* TX: Faith Clinic, n.d.

_____. *Power from on High.* TX: Faith Clinic, n.d.

_____. *The Grace of God in My Life.* TX: Faith Clinic, 1952.

_____. *When Prayer Fails*. TX: Grant's Faith Clinic, n.d.

Gray, Steve. *Hope Heals*. MO: World Revival Press, 2003.

Grensted, Rev. L. W. *Psychology and God: A Study of The Implications of Recent Psychology For Religious Belief and Practice.* London: Longmans, Green and Co., 1931.

_____. *The Person Of Christ.* London: Nisbet & Co., Ltd., 1933.

Harrell, Jr., David Edwin. *Oral Roberts: An American Life* San Francisco: Harper & Row Publishers, 1985.

Hayes, Norvell. *The Healing Handbook.* Tulsa, OK: Harrison House, 1982.

Heard, Gerald. *A Preface to Prayer*. NY: Harper & Brothers, 1934.

Heiler, Friedrich. *Prayer: A Study in the History and Psychology of Religion.* Oxford: Oneworld Publications, 1932.

Herman, E. *Creative Prayer.* London: James Clarke & Co., Ltd., 1921.

Hicks, Roger. *How to Read the Bible*. London: Moral Re-Armament, 1940.

Hickson, James Moore. *Heal The Sick.* London: Methuen & Co., 1924.

Holm, Nora Smith. *The Runner's Bible.* NY: Houghton Mifflin Company, 1913.

Inman, Philip. *Christ in the Modern Hospital*. London: Hodder & Stoughton Ltd., 1937.

James, William. *The Varieties of Religious Experience*. NY: First Vintage Press/The Library of America Edition, 1990.

*New Jerusalem Bible*

Jones, E. Stanley. *Christ And Human Suffering.* New York: The Abingdon Press, 1930.

_____. *The Christ of the Mount*. NY: Abingdon Press, 1930.

Jung, Carl Gustav. *Modern Man In Search of a Soul.* NY: Harcourt, Brace & World, Inc., 1933.

_____. *Psychology & Religion.* New Haven: Yale University Press, 1938.

_____. *The Psychogenesis of Mental Disease.* NY: Bolingen Foundation, 1960.

K., Mitchell. *How it Worked: The Story of Clarence H. Snyder and The Early Days of Alcoholics Anonymous in Cleveland, Ohio*: NY: AA Big Book Study Group, 1997.

K., Richard. *Early A.A. - Separating Fact From Fiction: How Revisionists Have Led Our History Astray*. Haverhill, MA: Golden Text Publishing Co., 2003.

Kagawa, Toyohiko. *Love: The Law of Life.* Philadelphia: The John C. Winston Company, 1929.

Kelsey, Morton T. *Psychology, Medicine & Christian Healing*. Rev. ed. San Francisco: Harper & Row, Publishers, 1966.

Kenyon, E. W. *Jesus the Healer.* Kenyon's Gospel Publishing Society, Inc., 2000.

_____. *The True Story*. FL: Creation House, 1997.

_____. *The Wonderful Name of Jesus.* Kenyon's Gospel Publishing Society, 1998.

*King James Version, Authorized*

King, J. D. *"Written Not With Ink But With the Spirit."* MO: World Revival Press, 2003

Kitchen, V. C. *I Was a Pagan.* NY: Harper & Brothers, 1934.
Kurtz, Ernest. *Not-God: A History of Alcoholics Anonymous*, Exp ed. Hazelden, 1991.
Lake, Dr. John G. Lake. *The Astounding Diary of Dr. John G. Lake*. TX: Christ for the Nations, 1987.
Laubach, Frank. *Prayer (Mightiest Force in the World*). NY: Fleming H. Revell, 1946.
Laymon, Charles M. *A Primer of Prayer*. Nashville: Tidings, 1949.
Lewis, C. S. *Miracles: How God Intervenes in Nature and Human Affairs*. NY: Collier Books, 1960.
Liardon, Roberts. *God's Generals*. Tulsa, OK: Albury Publishing, 1996.
_____. *John G. Lake: The Complete Collection Of His Life's Teachings.* Tulsa, OK: Alsbury Publishing, 1999.
Lindsay, Gordon. *John Alexander Dowie: Champion Of The Faith*. TX: Christ for the Nations, Inc., 1987.
_____. *John G. Lake: Apostle To Africa.* TX: Christ for the Nations, 2000.
_____. *The John G. Lake Sermons.* TX: Christ for the Nations, 2002
_____. *The New John G. Lake Sermons.* TX: Christ for the Nations, 1994.
_____. *William Branham: A Man Sent From God.* IN: William Branham Evangelistic Association, n.d.
Lovett, C. S. *Jesus Wants You Well!* Baldwin Park, CA: Personal Christianity, 1973.
Lupton, Dilworth. *Religion Says You Can.* Boston: The Beacon Press, 1938.
Macmillan, Ebenezer. *Seeking and Finding.* NY: Harper & Brothers, 1933.
Maillard, John. *Healing in the Name of Jesus.* London: Hodder & Stoughton, 1936.
Markey, Morris. *Alcoholics and God.* Liberty Magazine, 1939.
McCarthy, Katherine. *The Emmanuel Movement and Richard Peabody* (Journal of Studies on Alcohol, Vol. 45, No. 1, 1984).
McIntosh, Ron. *The Quest for Revival: Experiencing Great Revivals of the Past, Empowering You for God's Move Today.* Tulsa, OK: Harrison House, 1997.
Micklem, E. R. *Miracles & The New Psychology: A Study in the Healing Miracles of the New Testament.* London: Oxford University Press, 1922.
Moody, Dwight L. *Secret Power: Or, The Secret of Success in Christian Life and Work.* Chicago: F. H. Revell, 1881.
Mosely, Rufus. *Perfect Everything.* MN: Macalester Park Publishing, 1949.
Murch, James DeForest. *Successful C.E. Prayer-Meetings*. OH: Standard Publishing Co., 1930.
*New Bible Dictionary, Second Edition.* England: Inter-Varsity Press, 1982.
Newton, James Draper. *Uncommon Friends.* NY: Harcourt Brace, 1987.
Osborn, T.L. *Believers in Action.* Tulsa, OK: T. L. Osborn, 2000.
_____. *Healing the Sick.* Tulsa, OK: Harrison House, 1992.
_____. *Join This Chariot*. Tulsa, OK: Osborn Foundation, n.d.
_____. *Miracles: Proof of God's Power*. Tulsa, OK: Harrison House, 1981.
_____. Osborn, Daisy. *When Jesus Visited Our House*. Tulsa, OK: Faith Digest, 1960.
P. Wally. *But for the Grace of God.* WV: The Bishop of Books, 1995.
Parker, William R. and Elaine St. Johns. *Prayer Can Change Your Life.* New ed. NY: Prentice Hall, 1957.
*Pass It On.* NY: *Alcoholics Anonymous World Services*, 1984.

Paton, Wally. *How to Listen to God: A Guide to Successful Living Through the Practice of Two-way Prayer.* Tucson, AZ: Faith With Works Publishing Company, 2000.
Peabody, Richard R. *The Common Sense of Drinking.* Atlantic Monthly Press Book, 1939.
Peale, Norman Vincent. *The Positive Power of Jesus Christ.* NY: Foundation for Christian Living, 1980
_____. *The Power of Positive Thinking.* NY: Peale Center for Christian Living, 1978.
Peele, Stanton. *Diseasing of America.* Lexington, MA: Lexington Books, 1989.
_____. And Bufe, Charles. *Resisting 12-Step Coercion: How To Fight Forced Participation in AA, NA, or 12-Step Treatment.* Tucson, AZ: See Sharp Press, 1998.
Phillips, Rachel M. *Billy Sunday: Evangelist on the Sawdust Trail.* Barbour Books, 2001.
Pittman, Bill. *AA The Way It Began.* Seattle: Glen Abbey Books, 1988.
Pittman, Bill and B., Dick. *Courage to Change: The Christian Roots of the Twelve-Step Movement.* MN: Hazelden.
Poe, Stephen E. and Frances E. *A Concordance to Alcoholics Anonymous.* NV: Purple Salamander Press, 1990.
Pridie, J. R. *The Church's Ministry of Healing.* London: Society For Promoting Christian Knowledge, 1926.
Puller, F. W. *The Anointing of the Sick in Scripture and Tradition, with some Considerations on the Numbering of the Sacraments.* London: Society For Promoting Christian Knowledge, 1904.
Rawson, F. L. *The Nature of True Prayer.* England: The Society for Spreading The Knowledge of True Prayer, 1918.
Redwood, Hugh. *God in the Shadows.* London: Hodder & Stoughton, 1934.
Richardson, Alan. *The Miracle-Stories of the Gospels.* London: SCM Press Ltd, 1941.
Riss, Richard M. *A Survey of 20$^{th}$-Century Revival Movements in North America.* MA: Hendrickson Publishers, 1988.
Roberts, Oral. *Expect A Miracle: My Life and Ministry.* Nashville: Thomas Nelson Publishers, 1995.
_____. *If You Need Healing Do These Things.* Tulsa, OK: Healing Waters, Inc., 1952.
_____. *Oral Roberts' Life Story.* Tulsa, OK: Oral Roberts, 1952.
*Rotherham's Emphasized Bible.* MI: Kegel Publications, 1994.
S., Clarence. *Going through the Steps*, 2d ed. Altamonte Springs, FL: Stephen Foreman, 1985.
_____. *My Higher Power–The Lightbulb.* 2d ed., Altamonte Springs, FL: Stephen Foreman, 1985
Schaer, Hans. *Religion and The Cure of Souls in Jung's Psychology.* NY: Bolingen Foundation, 1950.
Schaff, Philip. *History of the Christian Church, Volume I,* 3$^{rd}$ Revision (Grand Rapids., MI: Wm B. Eerdman's Publishing Company, 1890.
Schambach, R. W. *Demon Possession Today and How to Be Free.* TX: Schambach Revivals, Inc., 1992.
_____. *God's Guarantee to Heal You.* Tx: Schambach Revivals, 1991.
_____. *The Price of God's Miracle-Working Power.* TX: Schambach Ministries, Inc., 1991.

*Second Reader for Alcoholics Anonymous.* Akron: AA of Akron, n.d.
Shafto, G. R.H. *The Wonders of the Kingdom: A Study of the Miracles of Jesus*. NY: George H. Doran Company, 1924.
Shoemaker, Helen Smith. *I Stand By The Door: The Life of Sam Shoemaker*. NY: Harper & Row Publishers, 1967.
Shoemaker, Samuel M., Jr. *Children of the Second Birth.* NY: Fleming H. Revell, 1927.
_____. *Confident Faith.* NY: Fleming H. Revell, 1932.
_____. *Extraordinary Living for Ordinary Men.* MI: Zondervan Publishing House, 1965.
_____. *How To Become A Christian*. NY: Harper & Row, Publishers, 1953.
_____. "How to Find God." *The Calvary Evangel*, July, 1957.
_____. *National Awakening*. NY: Harper & Brothers, 1936.
_____. *Realizing Religion.* NY: Association Press, 1923.
_____. *Religion That Works.* NY: Fleming H. Revell, 1928.
_____. *Sam Shoemaker at his best.* NY: Faith At Work, Inc., 1964.
_____. *The Church Can Save the World.* NY: Harper & Brothers, 1938
_____. *The Experiment of Faith*. NY: Harper & Brothers, 1957.
_____. *The Gospel According to You.* NY: Fleming H. Revell, 1934.
_____. *Twice-Born Ministers*. NY: Fleming H. Revell, 1929.
Smith, Bob and Sue Smith Windows. *Children of the Healer*. IL: Parkside Publishing, 1992.
Speer, Robert E. *Studies of the Man Christ Jesus*. NY: Fleming H. Revell, 1896.
_____. *The Principles of Jesus.* NY: Fleming H. Revell Company, 1902.
*Spiritual Milestones in Alcoholics Anonymous*. Akron: AA of Akron, n.d.
Stadsklev, Julius. *William Branham: A Prophet Visits South Africa*. MN: Julius Stadsklev, 1952.
Stafford, Tim. "The Hidden Gospel of the 12 Steps." *Christianity Today*, July 22, 1991.
Stalker, James. *The Life of Jesus Christ*. NY: Fleming H. Revell, 1891.
Streeter, B. H. *The God Who Speaks*. London: Macmillan & Co., Ltd., 1936.
Streeter, B. H. (Editor). *The Spirit: God and His Relation to Man Considered From The Standpoint of Philosophy, Psychology And Art.* London: Macmillan And Co., 1919.
Taylor, Vincent. *The Formation of the Gospel Tradition: Eight Lectures*. London: Macmillan & Co. Ltd., 1964.
Temple, William. *Christus Veritas: An Essay.* London: Macmillan & Co Ltd., 1954.
*The Book of Yahweh*, 7th ed.. Abilene, TX: The Houses of Yahweh, 1994.
*The Co-founders of Alcoholics Anonymous: Biographical sketches Their last major talks*, 1972, 1975.
*The Complete Parallel Bible.* Oxford: Oxford University Press, 1993.
*The Contemporary Parallel New Testament* (Eight Translations). NY: Oxford University Press, 1997.
*The Dead Sea Scrolls Bible*. HarperSanFrancisco, 1999.
*The Four Absolutes.* Cleveland: Cleveland Central Committee of A.A., n.d.
*The New Way of Life.* A.A. Cleveland: The Cleveland District Office of Alcoholics Anonymous, n.d.
*The Revised English Bible, New Testament.*
*The Schocken Bible: Volume I (The Five Books of Moses).* NY: Schocken Books, 1995.

*The Tidings*. March 24, 1943.
*The Upper Room* (Methodist quarterly periodical which began publishing in April, 1935).
Tileston, Mary W. *Daily Strength for Daily Needs*. Boston: Roberts Brothers, 1893.
Tournier, Paul. *The Healing of Persons*. NY: Harper & Row, Publishers, 1965.
_____. *The Person Reborn*. NY: Harper & Row, Publishers, 1966.
Towns, Elmer. Porter, Douglas. *The Ten Greatest Revivals Ever: From Pentecost to the Present*. MI: Servant Publications, 2000.
Troward, Thomas. *The Edinburgh Lectures on Mental Science*. NY: Dodd, Mead & Co., 1909.
*Vine's Expository Dictionary of Old and New Testament Words*. NY: Fleming H. Revell, 1981.
Walter, Howard A. *Soul Surgery*. Oxford: The Oxford Group, 1928.
Weatherhead, Leslie D. *Psychology and Life*. New York: Abingdon Press, 1935.
_____. *Psychology, Religion, and Healing*. NY: Abingdon-Cokesbury Press, 1951.
Weaver, C. Douglas. William Marrion Branham: The Healer-Prophet. GA; Mercer University Press, 2000.
Wells, Amos R. Expert Endeavor: A Text-book of Christian Endeavor Methods and *Principles*. Boston: United Society of Christian Endeavor, 1911.
*What Others Think of A.A.* Akron: Friday Forum Luncheon Club, circa 1941.
White, William L. *Slaying the Dragon: The History of Addiction Treatment and Recovery in America.* Bloomington, IL: Chestnut Health Systems/Lighthouse Institute, 1998.
Wigglesworth, Smith. *Smith Wigglesworth on Healing*. PA: Whitaker House, 1999.
Willitts, Ethel R. *Healing in Jesus Name*. Crawfordsville, IN: Ethel R. Willitts, Publisher, 1931.
Wilson, Jim. *Healing Through The Power of Christ*. London: James Clarke & Co., Ltd., 1946.
Wilson, Bill. *Bill Wilson's Original Story*. Bedford Hills, NY: Stepping Stones Archives, n.d., a manuscript whose individual lines are numbered 1 to 1180
Wilson, Lois. *Lois Remembers*. NY: Al-Anon Family Group Headquarters, 1987.
Wilson, W. G. *W. G. Wilson Reflections*. Bedford Hills, NY: Stepping Stones Archives, 1954.
Wing, Nell. *Grateful to Have Been There*. IL: Parkside Publishing Corporation, 1992.
Worcester, Elwood and Samuel McComb. *The Christian Religion as a Healing Power*. NY: Moffat, Yard And Company, 1909.
Worcester, Elwood and Samuel McComb, Isador H. Coriat. *Religion and Medicine: The Moral Control of Nervous Disorders*. New York: Moffat, Yard & Company, 1908.
*Young's Analytical Concordance*. Grand Rapids, MI: Robert Young, *n.d.*

## About Dick B.

Dick B. is an active, recovered member of Alcoholics Anonymous; a retired attorney; and a Bible student. He has sponsored more than one hundred men in their recovery from alcoholism. Consistent with A.A.'s traditions of anonymity, he uses the pseudonym "Dick B."

Dick is the father of two married sons (Ken and Don) and a grandfather. As a young man, he did a stint as a newspaper reporter. He attended the University of California, Berkeley, where he received his A.A. degree in economics with honors, and was elected to Phi Beta Kappa in his Junior year. In the United States Army, he was an Information-Education Specialist. He received his A.B. and J.D. degrees from Stanford University, and was Case Editor of the Stanford Law Review. Dick became interested in Bible study in his childhood Sunday School and was much inspired by his mother's almost daily study of Scripture. He joined, and later became president of, a Community Church affiliated with the United Church of Christ. By 1972, he was studying the origins of the Bible and began traveling abroad in pursuit of that subject. In 1979, he became much involved in a Biblical research, teaching, and fellowship ministry. In his community life, he was president of a merchants' council, Chamber of Commerce, church retirement center, and homeowners' association. He served on a public district board and was active in a service club.

In 1986, he was felled by alcoholism, gave up his law practice, and began recovery as a member of the Fellowship of Alcoholics Anonymous. In 1990, his interest in A.A.'s Biblical/Christian roots was sparked by his attendance at A.A.'s International Convention in Seattle. Since then, he has traveled widely; researched at archives, and at public and seminary libraries; interviewed scholars, historians, clergy, A.A. "old-timers" and survivors; and participated in conferences, programs, panels, and seminars on early A.A.'s spiritual history.

Dick B.'s body of work on the history and successes of early Alcoholics Anonymous includes seminars, books, articles, radio interviews, videos, audio cassettes tapes, and newspaper articles. They show how the basic, and highly successful, biblical ideas used by early AAs can be valuable tools for success in today's A.A. Also, the religious and recovery communities are using his research and titles to work more effectively with alcoholics, addicts, and others involved in Twelve Step programs.

He has had twenty-six titles, and more than 115 articles published about the history and successes of early A.A.: The titles are listed at the front of this volume and are described in much detail on the websites: http://www.dickb.com/titles.shtml; http://aa-history.com/bookstore.

These have been discussed in newspaper articles and reviewed in *Library Journal, Bookstore Journal, For A Change, The Living Church, Faith at Work, Sober Times, Episcopal Life, Recovery News, RecoveringTimes, Ohioana Quarterly, The PHOENIX, MRA Newsletter and the Saint Louis University Theology Digest.*

Dick now, and usually, has several works in progress. Much of his research and writing is done in collaboration with his older son, Ken, who holds B.A., B.Th., and M.A. degrees. Ken has been a lecturer in New Testament Greek at a Bible college and a lecturer in Fundamentals of Oral Communication at San Francisco State University. Ken is a computer specialist and a Director of Research and Marketing for Oahu Ethanol.

Dick is a member of the American Historical Association, Organization of American Historians, Research Society on Alcoholism, Alcoholism and Drugs History Society, Christian Association for Psychological Studies, Coalition of Prison Ministries, Association for Educational and Medical Research on Alcoholism, and International Substance Abuse and Addiction Coalition. He speaks at conferences, panels, seminars, and interviews.

Dick B.'s email address is: dickb@dickb.com. The URL address for his web site on the history and successes of early Alcoholics Anonymous is: http://www.dickb.com/index.shtml. His books can be purchased in bulk and at discounts through http://aa-history.com/bookstore.

# Order Form

# Catalog & Order Sheet

***** We suggest the entire 22-Volume Reference Set! *****

**How to Order the 22-Volume Set and/or Dick B.'s Individual Historical Titles on Early A.A.**

---

## Order Form

**Qty.**

| Qty. | Title | Price | |
|---|---|---|---|
| ____ | *Anne Smith's Journal, 1933-1939: A.A.'s Principles of Success (3rd ed.)* | $16.95 ea. | $______ |
| ____ | *By the Power of God: A Guide to Early A.A. Groups and Forming Groups Today* | $16.95 ea. | $______ |
| ____ | *Cured!: Proven Help for Alcoholics and Addicts* | $17.95 ea. | $______ |
| ____ | *Dr. Bob and His Library: A Major A.A. Spiritual Source (3rd ed.)* | $15.95 ea. | $______ |
| ____ | *God and Alcoholism: Our Growing Opportunity in the 21st Century* | $17.95 ea. | $______ |
| ____ | *Good Morning!: Quiet Time, Morning Watch, Meditation, and Early A.A. (2d ed.)* | $16.95 ea. | $______ |
| ____ | *Henrietta Seiberling: Ohio's Lady with a Cause* | $15.95 ea. | $______ |
| ____ | *Making Known the Biblical Roots of A.A.* | $24.95 ea. | $______ |
| ____ | *New Light on Alcoholism: God, Sam Shoemaker, and A.A. (2d ed.)* | $24.95 ea. | $______ |
| ____ | *That Amazing Grace: The Role of Clarence and Grace S. in A. A.* | $16.95 ea. | $______ |
| ____ | *The Akron Genesis of Alcoholics Anonymous (2d ed.)* | $17.95 ea. | $______ |
| ____ | *The Books Early AAs Read for Spiritual Growth (7th ed.)* | $15.95 ea. | $______ |
| ____ | *The Golden Text of A.A.: Early A.A., God, and Real Spirituality* | $14.95 ea. | $______ |
| ____ | *The Good Book and The Big Book: A.A.'s Roots in the Bible (2d ed.)* | $17.95 ea. | $______ |
| ____ | *The James Club* | $17.95 ea. | $______ |
| ____ | *The Oxford Group & Alcoholics Anonymous (2d ed.)* | $17.95 ea. | $______ |
| ____ | *Turning Point: A History of Early A.A.'s Spiritual Roots and Successes* | $29.95 ea. | $______ |
| ____ | *Twelve Step's for You* | $17.95 ea. | $______ |
| ____ | *Utilizing Early A.A.'s Spiritual Roots for Recovery Today* | $14.95 ea. | $______ |
| ____ | *When Early AAs Were Cured and Why* | $17.95 ea. | $______ |
| ____ | *Why Early A.A. Succeeded: The Good Book in A.A. Yesterday and Today* | $17.95 ea. | $______ |

Subtotal $________

[SPECIAL OFFER: Dick B.'s entire 22-volume set may be purchased for $250.00 plus $30.00 for Shipping & Handling (= $280.00 per set)] Qty.: _____ $______

Shipping and Handling (within the U.S.) **10% of retail (min. $4.50) $_______

Total Enclosed $________

Name:______________________________ (as it is on your credit card, if using one)

Address:_________________________________________________

City: _________________________State:________ Zip: _______________

CC Acct. #: ____________________________________ Exp.:__________

Tel.: _____________________________________

Signature: ____________________________________

Email: ______________________________________

** *Please contact us for Shipping and Handling charges for orders being shipped outside of the United States.*

No returns accepted. Please mail this Order Form, along with your check or money order (if sending one), to: Dick B., c/o Good Book Publishing Company, P.O. Box 837, Kihei, HI 96753-0837. Please make your check or money order payable to "Dick B." in U.S. dollars drawn on a U.S. bank. If you have any questions, please phone: 1-808-874-4876. Dick B.'s email address is: dickb@dickb.com. Dick B.'s web site on early A.A.'s history http://www.dickb.com/index.shtml

**Paradise Research Publications, Inc.**
P.O. Box 837
Kihei, HI 96753-0837
(808 874 4876)
Email: dickb@dickb.com
Internet URL address: http://www.dickb.com/index.shtml

ISBN 1-885803-94-X Price: $17.95